PETE

MY STORY

Pete Bennett

With Andrew Crofts

HarperCollins*Publishers*

HarperCollins*Publishers*
77–85 Fulham Palace Road,
Hammersmith, London W6 8JB

The HarperCollins website address is:
www.harpercollins.co.uk

First published by HarperCollins*Publishers* 2006

1 3 5 7 9 10 8 6 4 2

A catalogue record of this book is
available from the British Library

HB ISBN-13   978-0-00-725033-2
HB ISBN-10   0-00-725033-9
PB ISBN-13   978-0-00-725056-1
PB ISBN-10   0-00-725056-8

Printed and bound in Great Britain by
Clays Ltd, St Ives plc

Mixed Sources
Product group from well-managed
forests and other controlled sources
www.fsc.org Cert no. SW-COC-1806
© 1996 Forest Stewardship Council
FSC

INTRODUCTION

Being able to do this book is a brilliant opportunity, because I really want to try to explain to people what it feels like to be me. People have always made snap judgements about me. They might only have seen me walking down a crowded street, sitting in a school classroom or a pub, but that would be enough for them to decide that I was weird, or gay, or soft, or mad or very annoying, and I am excited to have an opportunity to paint a bit more of a detailed picture of how I got to be like I am.

I'm not the only person in the world with a few problems. Some people have far worse ones, and some have far milder ones. But we all start out from the same place, until things start happening to us. For some people the problems begin the first day they pop out into the world; for others, like me, they ambush us later on. When you see some guy walking down the street, talking to himself or shouting abuse at the gods, it's easiest to just cross the road and walk on by, but the chances are he didn't start out life like that. When he was born his mum and dad probably had very different plans for him, but stuff happened in his life, and probably in his head, that made him turn out different. It's not often someone like me really gets a chance to tell their story to a wide audience, rather than to just a few doctors, psychiatrists and so-called experts.

Maybe some kids will read this book, and then they might understand better why some of the other kids in the playground act a bit different to them. Maybe they'll feel it would be worth getting to know them better, rather than just shouting names and insults at them and knocking them down into the mud.

My mum's had a fair bit of superficial judgement landed on her over the years too; you know the sort of thing – a single busking mother with two sons by two different fathers, plus some pretty funky style decisions. She's got a bit of a mouth on her has Mum, and that hasn't always endeared her to everyone, particularly people in official positions who didn't quite get the whole Pete thing, but she still has the most gigantic circle of devoted friends, with me right at the front of the queue.

I hope there will be a few laughs along the way too, because we've laughed a lot over the years, when we weren't crying or shouting with frustration.

Anyway, this is it, for better or worse, my story.

CHAPTER ONE

A BIT OF A BAD START

I love my life, but it did get off to a bit of a dodgy start. I definitely wasn't keen to come out of Mum's belly. I probably felt safe and had a premonition of some of the stuff that was on its way once I hit the fresh air. I was about two weeks late popping out and Mum and Dad were sitting around in the hospital for a pretty long time, just waiting for me to decide I was ready to make my first dramatic entrance. Apparently there had been one giant explosion of a contraction and then just pure agony for Mum and no more action from me. I wasn't going anywhere. I stayed stuck there for the next seventeen hours, just couldn't get out, or didn't want to. I mean, why would I want to? Pretty cosy and safe in there, I should think.

I was taking so long getting my act together Dad got fed up with waiting and went home for his breakfast. Probably a bit of an attention-span problem going on there. I can understand that. I always have trouble sitting still waiting for something to happen.

A couple of foreign nurses, without too much English between them, were keeping Mum company, just watching the clock drag round, waiting for their shifts to end. One of them was so bored she was cleaning her ears out with a matchstick and examining the results before wiping it on the bedclothes.

'Ma babies all popped out like stones from peaches,' the other one kept saying, as if Mum was being deliberately lazy and messing up their day on purpose. 'Why don't you push, dahling?'

In the end an Egyptian lady-doctor sauntered into the room to see what was going on, or not going on, and realized that Mum was close to death. Suddenly everything changed, alarms started ringing and she was rushed off to the operating theatre. A few minutes later I was brought out on to centre stage by Caesarean.

So there I was, safely delivered and ready for whatever life might want to throw at me. A healthy eight pounds ten ounces and glad to be alive from the first moment I drew breath. No reason for anyone to worry there, baby delivered, job done, let's all go home. Mum put my surname down on the birth certificate as Bennett, because she believed Dad was going to marry her. To be fair to her he had asked, so she had every reason to be optimistic, but then he announced he was only joking. I suspect Mum didn't exactly roar with laughter at that one. His name isn't on my birth certificate at all because he didn't manage to turn up in time to sign it, having had a bit too much cider in the pub according to Mum. She generally tells it like it is, does Mum.

Mum hadn't realized she was pregnant with me till she was already five months gone. Apparently she'd been taking the Pill, but she had a dodgy Indian take-away one evening, and being sick must have shot the pill back up before it had done whatever it was supposed to do to discourage my conception. A bit of divine inter-vention there. I've always liked a good curry myself, and I am deeply indebted to the whole culinary species for my presence on Earth. If Mum had decided to have pasta or a McDonald's that night I guess I would never have happened.

So there I was, a bit of an unplanned event, although Mum assures me she'd always wanted me. She probably should have guessed she was pregnant a bit earlier, like the day when she felt violently sick on the bus, jumped off and threw up all over the window of a carpet showroom, under the furious gaze of half a dozen disgusted shop assistants. Mum was a full-fledged, scary-looking punk rocker at that stage, so it must have looked like a bit of a political statement, spewing up over a bourgeois retail outlet. They probably thought she had done it on purpose.

Mum is a really brilliant musician and it's not just me, her proud son, who thinks that. She went to the

Guildhall School of Music and Drama for four years, studying to become a concert violinist. Despite all the piercings and the spiky, multicoloured hair, leather clothes and fishnets, she was always very serious about her work and her art. She was really good at the violin, won a scholarship and everything, and she loved classical music, but it was punk music she really loved to listen to – Billy Idol alongside Yehudi Menuhin. She must have stuck out among the other young prodigies like a septic finger.

There was only one other punk in the college, an opera singer called Anna, who was Mum's best friend and Rod Steiger's daughter. Steiger was one of the biggest Hollywood stars of his day (he was the one in the famous scene with Marlon Brando in *On the Waterfront*, in which Brando's character says 'I coulda been a contender...' He was playing Brando's brother). Anna's mum was the actress Claire Bloom, who had also trained at the Guildhall.

Mum was always short of money and had to make as much cash as she could at the beginning of her career by busking around the streets of London, meeting very different types to the ones studying at the Guildhall, and loving it. There was a pub on the corner of Oxford Street and Tottenham Court Road called the Tottenham, under the towering shadow of Centrepoint, where a lot of the alternative music people used to go at the beginning of the Eighties, people like Boy George who hadn't yet made it big with Culture Club, and the girls who would later become the hit group Bananarama. None of them had become stars by then and hung around the pub planning their big breakthroughs. Mum and the other buskers used to meet in the Diamond Dive, a little spit-and-sawdust concert hall downstairs at the Tottenham, to take acid, play music and socialize. That was where she met my dad.

'I was going in there one lunch time,' is how she explains it to me, 'and there was this gorgeous-looking punk standing outside, six foot two and like a cross between Adam Ant and Billy Idol, spiky black hair – the most gorgeous bloke I'd ever seen. So I pinched his leather-clad arse as I went past. I didn't think I had a chance in a million of going out with him. "Hello Gorgeous," I said and to my amazement he started chatting me up.'

They had a drink and Dad asked her if she wanted to go out with him for a proper date that night. They agreed to meet by the jukebox at 7.30, and when she got there she found another friend, a gay New Romantics fan called Scottish John, sitting at the same table. She was eagerly telling him about her date, and found out he was also waiting for a hot date. Both of them were in a state of high excitement and it wasn't until Dad came strutting over in all his glory that they realized they were both waiting for the same bloke. It turned out Dad had a bit of a warped sense of humour and had been watching them talking from across the room. Scottish John wasn't too happy to find out he was being wound up, because Dad wasn't gay, but at least it meant Mum got her date that night. He was called Mark Bennett and the rest of the evening must have gone well because they became a couple.

Mum was living in a squat at the time, and Dad had a room in Brockley in south-east London, so it made sense for her to move in with him. He might have had a roof over his head, but Dad didn't have much of a plan for how he was going to make a living, apart from having a strong belief that sooner or later a film producer was going to spot him walking down the road, would see his potential and turn him into a film star. Funnily enough, it did actually happen in a way when Derek Jarman, a famous avant-garde gay filmmaker of the time, did spot him in the street, took him home to his flat and got him pissed. Jarman had made a famous film about punks called *Jubilee*, starring Toyah Wilcox and Adam Ant, so this could have been the moment Dad had been waiting for. Unfortunately he had a bit too much to drink, puked all over the great director's carpet and got thrown out, so he missed his big chance. (It did at least mean he preserved his honour, of course.)

He and Mum must have made a formidable-looking couple. They both loved to dress up and sometimes he would even paint a white stripe across his nose, making himself look even more like Adam Ant. He was definitely a man of his time, and a bit of a peacock.

Earning the money, however, was down to Mum, so she used to busk with her friends Gini and Carolyn around the tube stations, calling themselves Humouresque. Green Park was the best site and they took turns there with all the other acts vying for the attention of tourists, shoppers and day-trippers, trying to collect as many coins as possible before the end of their shift. Business wasn't too bad, partly because they were really good and partly because the sight of three outrageous punk girls playing classical music was new. Years later Nigel Kennedy, the renowned soloist, told Mum he'd got the whole idea for his own famously scruffy image from watching them when they appeared on the *Russell Harty Show*.

I don't remember anything about Dad at that time to be honest. Mum says he was a bit mental. He used to be able to talk in dozens of voices at once, like Robin Williams does in the Disney version of *Aladdin*, when he plays the genie. I can do that too, so maybe I take after him in more ways than just looking like him. Maybe Dad had a touch of the Tourette's, even if he didn't have the tourettey movements like I have. Once you start looking for Tourette's you can end up seeing bits of it in pretty much everyone, especially men.

He certainly wasn't much good at getting jobs in those days. He tried being a milkman, but gave that up. He did have a typewriter though, and used to put a lot of time into composing letters of complaint about products and sending them off to the manufacturers concerned in the hope of getting some offer of compensation. That particular business venture didn't meet with much success and so Mum's busking was still all they had to live on. And once I was born poor old Mum still had to fork out for babysitters out of her money because Dad was always mysteriously too busy to look after me for her.

I guess they were never a match made in heaven. They'd even got a bit pissed off with each other during the pregnancy and Mum had stormed off and got another flat with Gini, which immediately made Dad want her back. While I was turning into a full-sized bump inside her she was living in a room in Queensway, being harassed by a nasty Greek landlord who wanted to get her and Gini out. He smashed a plate glass window, poisoned the goldfish, put superglue in the locks and tried all the tricks he could think of to make life unbearable for them, but Mum was not one to be intimidated easily. She didn't intend to be put out on the streets with a foetus inside her, so she wrote a letter to her MP and got allotted a council flat in Peckham. She and Dad decided to give their relationship another shot and he moved back in with her to be there for my arrival and to have a go at the whole happy families thing.

While she was waiting for me to arrive Mum wanted to call me Sebastian, after a line in a song by Cockney Rebel, but she changed her mind once I was actually there.

'You'd been through such hell coming out and you seemed so calm about it all,' she told me later, when I was old enough to understand. 'I remembered something from my Catholic childhood about St Peter being called "the Rock", so I thought I'd call you after him.'

So that was me, 'St Peter, the Rock', finally out into the world and ready to roll in Peckham, deep in the heart of South London.

CHAPTER TWO

ROCK AND ROLL BABY

It started to look like Mum's career was going to save the family finances. Siouxsie and the Banshees, who were a big post-punk and goth band at the time (they had also starred in Derek Jarman's *Jubilee* film), asked her and her friends to go on tour with them. Siouxsie, who came from the same Bromley area as David Bowie, had always been controversial, wearing bondage and fetish gear on stage and getting into trouble at one time for wearing swastika armbands. The Banshees were a huge influence on a lot of other acts that followed. This was a big-name group and they were going to pay Mum £490 for ten days' work, which was a lot since Dad had so far only managed to get about £17-worth of vouchers out of all his letter writing. I was around nine months old by then, so Dad thought he might be able to cope with looking after me. He got his mum in to help him and, as far as I can remember, nothing drastic went wrong, although they probably wouldn't have told Mum if it had.

Then Mum got a booking to play with Marc Almond and Soft Cell for a night at Drury Lane, having met Marc at the Batcave, a gothic club just off Carnaby Street in Soho, where a lot of the punk music people were choosing to spend their nights off.

Mum and Dad had a bit of a row over her paying for a babysitter for the night and it ended with Dad making off to the pub with the money allocated for the babysitter, leaving me rolling gently down the hill in my buggy with Mum running after me. I think that was probably the moment when Mum decided it was time to have a go at being a single mother. Not too sure whether Dad walked out or was kicked out, but he definitely wasn't around any more after that. His disappearance didn't have any great effect on me at the time since there were always plenty of other interesting-looking people lurking about in our lives to look after me and distract me from the spontaneous combustion of my nuclear family unit.

Mum and I spent a lot of time with Marc Almond back then because Gini ended up marrying Dave Ball, who was the other part of Soft Cell, and Mum started living with their manager, Steve Ø, who had lots of other successful acts on his books at the time as well. That particular relationship didn't last that long, I think, although her friendship with Marc Almond has lasted a lifetime.

Despite the starry names she was working for, the gigs were only sporadic, not enough to ensure there was food on the table every day of the week, so Mum and her mates still had to keep going with the busking when the cash ran out. They used to take me with them sometimes, popping me in the buggy and letting me conduct along to the music in the hope of attracting a few more coins to fall into their violin cases. Apparently I was always happy and laughing as a baby and willing to go along with whatever was happening, so I was probably a bit of an asset in the 'cutes' department. There's nothing like a cheerful-looking kid to get the donations flowing in. It was my first taste of performance art and I had no complaints about all the attention I was getting either.

I even went on the *Russell Harty Show* with them and had my picture taken with Pat Phoenix, who was the big soap opera star of the day, famous for playing Elsie Tanner in *Coronation Street* (sort of like the Barbara Windsor of her day). Anthony Booth, Tony Blair's father-in-law, was on the bill too, being one of the stars of the comedy series, *Till Death Us Do Part*. Russell Harty was a sort of camp version of Michael Parkinson and his show was one of the biggest chat shows in the country, a bit like getting invited on to *Jonathan Ross* these days. The most famous moment was when the androgynous New York model and disco diva, Grace Jones, slapped him around the head on air for turning his back on her in order to talk to another guest.

Mum and her group would do a lot of street entertaining in Covent Garden as well. She used to dress up as a bee to play 'Flight of the Bumble Bee' and stuff like that. When there was a competition to find the 'Busker of the

Year' the only people who were better than them were a six-piece band called The Vulcans, who used to wear white coats and clown around singing funny songs. Mum and I used to go everywhere with them and I became like their group mascot. They would use cardboard boxes as a drum kit and I would hide inside one of the boxes so that I could spring out at the end, like Marilyn Monroe coming out of President Kennedy's birthday cake. The audience loved it and I loved their applause and their laughter. One of the Vulcans used to do a song about a thick bloke called 'Neanderthal Man', while playing a ukulele and wearing a silly hat. One day, hungry for another dose of the lime-light, I climbed on to his foot and clung to his leg like a little monkey as he dragged me around behind him, still singing. It went down so well with the crowd that they kept it in the act. I was carving out a career for myself before I even knew what a career was.

When the guys in the Vulcans found out that Mum and I were going to be on our own for Christmas one year they invited us to spend it with them in Portsmouth. We drove down to the coast in the back of their van, singing songs and bouncing around on blankets, since there weren't any seats. We all went on an outing to the torture museum on Christmas Day. There was an implement for screwing down a woman's tongue so she couldn't talk – a bit harsh, I thought, but very interesting!

Another day we all watched a video of *Grease* together, three times in a row, singing along to the songs. It immediately became my favourite movie. It was nice to sing some new songs because most of the time Mum and I would be pogoing round the flat on our own to Billy Idol's *Whiplash Smile* album. 'Dancing with Myself' had been both Mum and Dad's favourite record even before they met, and constant exposure made it mine too.

Mum had another interesting friend called Johny, who was in a goth group called Band of Holy Joy. He stole a gravestone, complete with stone angel, and gave it to Mum as a birthday present one night. Neither of us was too keen to have it in the house, so we smuggled it back into the graveyard together the next day.

When I was three or four, Mum was invited to join a theatre company called Impact and travel to Italy with them. Apparently the Italians are very into fringe theatre. The organizers said I could come too because there were going to be a couple of other small children in the troupe and so they were planning to take a childminder with them. Mum leapt at the opportunity and we spent six months touring around the north of Italy in the summer. I learnt to climb trees and they had an old broken record player that I was allowed to mess around with. We all lived together in a communal house in the middle of some lettuce fields. I wish I could remember more about it, it sounds like the most idyllic childhood summer possible when Mum describes it, but I have to rely on her version because my memories have mostly been blown away by events since then.

I always loved watching Mum on stage. She appeared in something called *The Magical Olympic Games* at the National Theatre on London's South Bank, and she did a lot at the Institute of Contemporary Arts in Pall Mall, just down the road from Buckingham Palace. I was constantly boasting about her to anyone who would listen; still am, as you may have noticed. No one else I knew had a mum who did such great stuff or hung out with such weird and famous people. Every kid watched *Top of the Pops* in those days, but not many could point to one of their parents on the screen.

She was really versatile, appearing with Paul Weller at Wembley one day and playing with the Royal Philharmonic Orchestra the next. She could play anything. She was always having themed parties, like gypsy or Spanish, where all her friends would dress up and they would play music that went with the food, raising money for charities. She was often on *Top of the Pops* or *The Tube*, playing with The Cure or Texas or the Smashing Pumpkins. They don't let kids into those television recordings, something to do with insurance, so I used to have to watch her on the telly just like everyone else. It made me so proud.

Carolyn, the other member of Humouresque, went off to play with Fun Boy Three, and then Mum got hired by the Communards, who were big at the time, having had 'Don't Leave Me This Way' at number one in the charts for weeks. Their lead singer was Jimmy Somerville, who was one of the first gay pop stars to come out of the closet and had a really distinctive falsetto singing voice. I loved hanging out with him and used to call him 'Auntie Jessie'. Mum had to take me with her on one of their two-week tours because her childminder let her down, and the coach driver, John, used to look after me while the rest of them were on stage performing. The bus was always full of lesbians and poofs and the band's cloney friends, and I was always the centre of attention. I mean, how cool is it to be on the road with a rock band even before your first day at school?

Mum had had a varied and dramatic childhood herself. My Grandad had been working as a civil servant in London when he decided he wanted a better life for his four kids than a council flat in Wandsworth, so he got transferred to Bristol and bought a little house in the country for them all to live in. He was keen on the idea of women getting an education and Mum was bright and did well at school, so it all went well until she was sixteen and she and Grandad fell out. Two powerful characters meeting one another head on, I guess: lots of middle-aged testosterone and adolescent hormones flying around and neither of them willing to give way. It ended up with Mum being chucked out of the house and spending a couple of years living rough, sleeping under the pier in Weston-super-Mare, or on other people's floors until some friends of the family took her under their wing and helped her fulfil her dream of going to the Guildhall. Maybe that experience was the reason why she didn't go completely mad when she found out how I was living later on in Brighton. She'd been through the same thing herself and knew that there are worse things than not having a home of your own when you're young and finding your way in the world. People worry too much about where they are going to sleep each night; something usually turns up.

Mum was a bit of a romantic right from the start, always dreaming of how life should be, but things never quite seemed to work out right for her in the early days. Maybe she was just a bit too feisty for her own good. But if she hadn't been so feisty maybe she wouldn't have survived all the ordeals that were to come, and maybe she wouldn't have fought so hard to get me a fair deal when everything started to go wrong.

The council estate Mum and I were living on in Peckham was a bit rough. I guess it was the sort of place the council put people who they had to house in a hurry (people like my punky single-mum for a start). Other people on the estate weren't always quite as capable of keeping things together as she was. Quite a few of them had pretty much totally lost the plot.

There was a nine-year-old kid living a few flats down, for instance, who used to come knocking on the door each day begging for food. He was looking after his eight younger brothers and sisters because his mum and dad were both alcoholics and not much good for anything. Mum would always give him something, and one time we went down to their flat for some reason. I was shocked to see how they were living, with pigeons roosting in the bedroom. Most of the kids were naked, rolling around on the floor, not even speaking properly, just grunting at one another like they had been transported through time from the Stone Age. Even when they were dressed their clothes stank of piss.

Their mum came round one evening and told us her husband had been taken into hospital and asked Mum to look after all the kids for her while she went to visit him. She didn't reappear till the next day, by which time Mum and I had rummaged through all my old clothes and found new stuff for them to wear while their own clothes went through the washing machine, several times. One of the girls had knickers that were so old they disintegrated when she took them off. Her mum accused Mum of stealing them once she got her home and discovered they were missing. It turned out the dad hadn't been to the hospital at all; they'd just gone down the pub together.

Everyone on the estate was fed up with the family's constant begging and after a while their flat was burnt out and they had to be re-housed in a new area where they could start afresh. The mother came back to visit us later and told us that the smallest baby had died of an ear infection. I was really upset, having looked after it for that day and got to know it.

'Ah,' she casually dismissed my tears. 'I can always have another one.'

The dad took a bit of a fancy to Mum and came to the door having tried to drown out the smell of unwashed clothes and beer with gallons of cheap after-shave, and told her he had £110 saved in the bank and thought they should get together. Mum went mad, yelling at him that if he had that kind of money he should be spending it on his children, not on trying to get his end away. I was shocked, I'd never seen her so angry about anything. I was really glad I had her to look after me rather than some of the other women I saw around the place.

CHAPTER THREE

BABY MINDERS

Mum's biggest problem, once she had me, was finding affordable babysitters when she went to work. I don't think people ever minded having me because I was always a pretty happy kid, but most people around our way had enough trouble caring for their own children, never mind someone else's. There was a lovely Indian family who I used to stay with quite a lot. Mum even bought a set of bunks so I could sleep over there without putting any of them out of their beds. Their mum was called Rosen and she made great curries.

Mum took me out with Rosen's kids one day and a white van driven by a couple of men cruised past. One of them leant out the window and shouted abuse at us, assuming we were all Mum's children, spitting at her before accelerating off. I couldn't understand why anyone would be so horrible to a woman with small children. Mum tried to explain to me about racism and how some people hated other people simply because they had different-coloured skins. I remember it making me feel sad, but also puzzled because I really liked people who were different and new, interesting and surprising. I liked Rosen's family because the women wore swathes of brightly coloured fabric and their house was full of exotic smells. I liked the way they talked with their musical-sounding accents and the pictures they had on their walls.

Bit by bit over the coming years I learnt about the National Front and their hatred of anyone who wasn't like them. At the same time I was aware I was also growing to be more different, and therefore more vulnerable, myself. Mostly I liked the way I was, but I didn't always like the reactions I got from other people.

When I was about four, Mum went on another short tour with the Communards, and left me with a different local family for a few days. When she came back she found me playing on my own in the car park outside their house. The lady who was supposed to be looking after me had left her front door open so she could watch me, but had fallen asleep on the sofa. Mum went berserk, ranting and raving that anything could have happened to me while she slept. She must have been very torn between her need to make money, her love of music and performing, and her maternal urge to look after me herself all the time.

The same family had a pit bull terrier. I always loved dogs and wanted to cuddle them all the moment I saw them, but this mean bastard had other ideas as I threw my arms around its neck, and sank its teeth into my face. Luckily it missed my eye but it ripped open my top lip and there was blood everywhere. Mum was there at the time and rushed me down to the hospital, where we sat for several hours with her holding my lip on, waiting for the surgeon. I was shaking uncontrollably and crying but Mum always stayed incredibly quiet and calm in these crises, although she fainted dead away once the whole thing was over.

When the surgeon did eventually get round to us Mum and four nurses had to lie across my body to stop me fighting him off as he set to work with his needle and thread. She made them put in an extra stitch after they thought they had finished because she was so determined I wouldn't end up scarred, which didn't endear her to them, or me at the time. Despite her best efforts there's still a tiny scar, but you can hardly see it.

The babysitting problem was eventually solved by the intervention of Mum's cousin, Poofy-Cousin-Marcus, who had already helped bring up his brother's four kids when his brother was away at sea, so he knew what he was doing when it came to nappy changing, kids' meals and nursery school runs. He was totally happy mincing around the kitchen all day, scrubbing and bleaching. He stayed with us on and off for years and I caught him slipping money under my pillow when my first tooth came out and was convinced from then on that the tooth fairy was a balding poof with glasses and painted-on eyebrows. He was great, throwing himself into the role of nanny with gusto and filling all my criteria for being different, interesting and funny. He was completely happy gossiping with the mothers at the school gates, or showing off how white he had managed to get the wash that day.

'Mmmm,' I heard him purring at a neighbour who was pegging out her washing on her balcony one day. 'Yours haven't come up quite so white this week, have they, love?'

One of his boyfriends broke his heart while he was living with us and he disappeared into his bed for about a week, unable to face the world. As it was his birthday, Mum and I sorted him out a cake with a candle to cheer him up, taking it in to his bedroom. He emerged from under the sheets to blow the candle out.

'So,' Mum said. 'Make a wish.'

'I wish I was dead,' he shrieked, whipping the sheets back over his head.

I remember going into his bedroom once and pulling his bedclothes off to wake him up, just as he let out a gigantic fart. Cool!

Mum continued to take me on tour with her from time to time. We went to Germany for six months with a band called Rausch when I was about six. They were a very dark bunch, surrounded by lots of drugs, which Mum didn't like. She was always lecturing me about not doing drugs, especially cocaine, which she said made people sadistic and cold and evil. It wasn't a particularly happy time for Mum but I enjoyed myself. I always enjoyed myself. We were in Berlin just before the Wall came down and the whole world changed in one night. Mum had been predicting it would happen, having seen it in a vision. I remember watching it coming down on the news and knowing it was important because everyone was talking about it and celebrating, but I didn't really understand why. What was a Communist?

One of the band members in Germany really took to me and would laugh every time he saw me, calling me 'Charlie'.

'Why are you calling him Charlie?' Mum wanted to know. 'His name's Pete.'

'Because he is like Charlie Chaplin.'

He wasn't the last person to say that and I liked the fact that I could make people laugh by clowning around. It always felt good to be the centre of attention, particularly if it was happy attention. All the world loves a clown.

CHAPTER FOUR

A VISIT FROM AN ANGEL

I was always a bit of a daydreamer, drifting off into a world of my own whenever there wasn't anything going on that was interesting enough to hold my attention. I didn't see a problem with it, still don't. I think it's good to be able to keep yourself entertained inside your head, but sometimes it can get you into trouble – in school classrooms, for instance, or when you are meant to be doing something other people think is important.

I was supposed to get the bus home from school so Mum could meet me off it at the other end. One day I simply forgot to get on, because I was so distracted with my own thoughts and with watching whatever was going on in the street around me. When all the other kids poured out and trotted off to meet their waiting mothers, Mum realized with a sinking heart that I wasn't among them and immediately freaked out, convincing herself I'd been abducted by a paedophile ring (a common fear among mothers of temporarily missing children, I guess). She ran to find a friend of hers, a disabled woman who was able to drive, and begged her to give her a lift up to the school to search for me. The poor flustered woman rushed out in her wheelchair and they piled into the car together.

Mum was trying to keep calm and allow her friend the time she needed to get going, but pictures of all the things that could have happened to me were crowding into her brain, making her a bit frantic. By the time they were on the road she had managed to panic her friend so much that she crashed the car, smashing the windscreen and dissolving into tears at her failure to complete the mission to rescue gallant Little Pete from the 'evil paedos'. At that point Mum abandoned all pretence at being patient, leapt out and legged it the rest of the way on her own, leaving her friend shaking and crying in the car. When she found me happily wandering around the school playground humming to myself, staring up at the sky, she was not pleased. I think she might even have given me a bit of a swipe around the back of the legs to try to wake me up a bit.

Although I didn't know anything about it at the time, the stress of touring and feeling guilty about leaving me, plus all the worry about money, was getting Mum down, and around this time she had a nervous breakdown. She became convinced she'd met the Devil and she had some sort of religious conversion back to the Catholic Church that she'd been brought up in. As far as I was concerned we had just made a whole new set of nice friends down at the local church.

A couple of religious Irish women then frightened her by accusing her of condemning me to hell by not getting me baptized. She was due to go on tour in Japan with an Indie rock band called the Woodentops the next day and she was terrified something would happen to me while she was away and I would go straight to hell and damnation before she had time to do anything about saving me. Unable to get a priest to come out in the middle of the night to perform the ceremony, she baptized me herself while I was asleep. I wasn't aware of what she was doing but while she was splashing around my bedroom with some holy water she'd mixed up herself, I had a dream in which I saw a huge golden angel.

'From now on you have to take my name,' the angel told me. 'My name is Michael.'

It was a really cool dream, and I told Mum about it before she set off for the plane the next morning, leaving me in the care of Poofy-Cousin-Marcus. On the way to the airport she stopped off at the church to find someone to tell her who the angel Michael was.

'That would be the Archangel Michael,' a man told her. 'He's the one who led the fight against the Devil in the beginning of time.'

Since she was still convinced she had been having some personal trouble with the Devil, this put her mind at rest a bit, although she was still feeling bad about leaving me so much. I can still remember that dream vividly, even today when so many other memories have vanished, and for ages afterwards I would draw pictures of the Angel Michael, although I started to add wings to make him conform a little more to stereotype. Although he didn't have any wings in the dream, he was surrounded by a heavenly golden light, which was how I knew for sure that he was an angel. From then on I took Michael as my middle name. Later a priest insisted on baptizing me again himself, not willing to accept Mum's DIY version as the real thing, but it wasn't as good as when Mum did it, and I didn't get to dream of any angels that time.

I've always been good at drawing. It's just something I'm able to do. When I was about two I drew a picture called 'The Shouting Man', a bit like a primitive version of 'The Scream' by Edvard Munch. It was an oval shape with a vortex for where the mouth should be, quite scary and angry-looking, a bit like a baby having a wailing tantrum, which was something I never did myself. Maybe I was holding the anger in, even at that age, and the picture was the only way for it to escape. Now I am 'the shouting man' for real, letting everything out all the time, unable to bottle anything up inside for long, so maybe I was having premonitions even then of what was to come. Maybe there was already something taking root inside my head, a troublesome thought behind the façade of the cheerful, amiable little boy. If there was I have no memory of it.

When I had difficulty attracting Mum's attention to what I was saying because she was so preoccupied with her worries, I used to draw the shouting man and wave the picture in front of her, the words 'Mum! Mum!' coming out of his mouth in a bubble, like in the comics I read.

Mum showed the picture to a friend once.

'You should be ashamed,' the friend told her. 'What kind of a terrible mother are you? Imagine having a kid who has to draw a picture just to get your attention.'

I didn't want to make her feel guilty; I just wanted to be noticed. I thought she was a great mum – she always called me her little 'Peter Bumpkin'. I just wanted to talk to her and tell her about all the stuff that was going on in my head. But all kids do that, don't they? They burble on in a constant stream of consciousness while the adults around them zone out and give the odd grunt in response in order to give the impression that they're listening.

I don't know how I became Bumpkin with a 'b' because it started with a nursery rhyme.

Peter, Peter, Pumpkin Eater
Had a wife but couldn't keep her.
So he put her in a pumpkin shell
And there he kept her very well.

Teachers were always singling out my pictures and telling me they had never seen anything like it for a child of my age. It was nice to be good at something, but I couldn't really take credit for it because it was a natural talent. I didn't have to work at it or anything; I could just do it. The pictures were clear in my head and my hands were able to reproduce them on paper. I remember a green painting, all covered in tadpoles, which I did when I was about five, which everyone thought was brilliant. I always feel calm when I'm drawing, as if everything is right in my universe.

Pushed into a corner by her breakdown, Mum decided she had to choose between rock and roll and bringing me up properly as a full-time mother. So rock and roll got the push for a few years and Mum joined a folk group at the local church so she could keep up with her music and be with me. During her breakdown she had been seeing a series of numbers flashing in her head all the time, popping up everywhere she went. She couldn't understand what they meant but when she walked into the church for the first time she saw the same numbers on the hymn board, like a sign telling her that she was on the right path and had arrived at the right destination. We've both had a lot of those sorts of experiences, lots of visions, premonitions and signs, some of them spooky, some of them shocking, some of them really comforting.

Mum seemed to just want to disappear during that period, as if she didn't want anyone to look at her or be attracted to her. She would deliberately wear boring clothes, which was a radical move for a woman who used to change the colour of her hair as often as most people change their knickers. I quite liked the God Squadders she was hanging out with now, even though they were incredibly straight compared to us and the sort of people we had hung out with before. They all seemed to be dead keen to save our souls from eternal damnation, which was kind of them.

We went on a pilgrimage with them one year, walking in the rain all the way from Epping to Walsingham in Norfolk where there is a famous shrine to the Virgin Mary. They call it 'England's Nazareth', apparently. The shrine had been there since 1061, even before William the Conqueror. (See how educational the trip was?) Anyway, we had to take turns carrying this great big cross, and I got to have my go as well, walking barefoot on the wet roads like some dramatic biblical figure. I loved it, even though the walking made my knees swell. It took four days and we had to carry our rucksacks and sleeping bags on our backs. I loved the whole travelling experience, out on the open road with its constantly changing scenery, part of a friendly group of people.

The only thing I didn't like was all the dead animals we passed. Every dead bird or squashed hedgehog would have me crying for miles, and when we came across the skeleton of a deer I was beside myself, thinking of Bambi's mother being killed by the hunters in the forest. It was the first time I had been faced with mortality and it made me uneasy.

When we finally got to Walsingham the shrine was lit by thousands of candles and looked magical and otherworldly. I just stood and stared at all the little flames flickering in the shadows, basking in the quietness and coolness inside the ancient walls.

The first Christmas after Mum had joined the church, when she was still feeling too fragile emotionally even to go busking, she warned me that we weren't going to be able to afford any presents, or even a proper Christmas lunch that year. I think I was a bit disappointed, but not mortified. Then the day before Christmas Eve a couple of elderly ladies from the church came knocking on the door with a hamper. They told us they had a list of the needy living in the area who they distributed these gifts to and they had decided we would be worthy recipients. I think Mum was a bit shocked to think that we looked that desperate, but she was still too grateful for the hamper to protest. The moment they'd gone we were excitedly tearing it open and Mum was weeping with joy at the sight of so much food. It had everything we could need for the celebration, from the turkey to mince pies and Christmas pudding.

Although I liked the people at the church, I wasn't quite sure about the whole believing-in-God thing. I was quite willing to believe in angels, since I had actually met one, and happy to keep an open mind, but I can't say I exactly had 'faith' in a way any priest would have approved of. The question I decided I wanted to ask God, if I ever got to meet him, was how did he make himself. A variation of the old chicken-and-egg and which-came-first puzzle, I guess. When I did finally get to meet him, many years later, I forgot to ask the question in all the excitement. I wasn't quite sure, either, why we had to stare at statues dripping with blood when we were at school. That part of it all seemed a bit spooky to me.

Most of the Christian meetings we went to happened in a nearby fourth-floor council flat, where the leader of the group lived. When he moved to a house closer to the church Mum and I went round to clean the flat up for the next tenants. When they arrived they were really scary, the complete opposite to the clean, sober Christians before them. I couldn't stop myself from staring, open-mouthed, every time we went round there. The mother of the family was huge and smelly and had no teeth because, she told us, her husband had knocked them out with a baseball bat. The family had a couple of evil-looking Dobermans, called Satan and Lucifer, which they never took out of the flat, allowing them to crap and piss wherever they wanted indoors. The dogs suited their names perfectly, true hounds of hell, always growling under their breath and watching me out of the corners of their eyes as if waiting for their chance to pounce. The flat got to such a state that the dog pee was seeping through the ceilings on to the neighbours below, dripping down their walls. The family had a son, who wanted to be my friend. He had a big dent in his head.

'What happened to your head?' I asked.

'The telly fell on it,' he informed me.

Another neighbour's husband died and everyone clubbed together to buy a big wreath of flowers to display in his memory on the landing outside the flats. My new-found, dent-headed friend was caught nicking it and trying to squeeze it in through his mother's front door.

My real best friend at the time was Leon from upstairs and we used to play with our He-Man dolls together, or dress up as Spiderman (or Darth Vader once I was hooked on *Star Wars*). Leon's mum was really nice too, and had a successful job of some sort, which made other people on the estate so jealous of her they eventually torched her car. We went to CenterParcs together for a holiday, just like two normal families.

Things were seldom normal back at the flats. One morning, at about six o'clock when it was just getting light, Mum and I heard screams and gunshots outside. Mum phoned the police and we crouched together on the balcony, watching through the railings as police cars screeched into the courtyard below. The place was deserted apart from one lone black man who looked like he was peacefully making his way to work. The police all leapt on him, pummelling him to the ground.

'That's not fair,' I whispered to Mum. 'He's not doing anything wrong.'

'I'm going to say something,' Mum said, standing up to shout some sort of abuse at the police (she'd had a few run-ins with them herself while out busking and wasn't a huge fan). Just at that moment, however, they pulled a sawn-off shotgun out from under the man's coat and Mum sank quietly back down next to me. Apparently he'd shot some woman in the block over a drugs deal that had gone wrong.

The local papers that week said that the arrest had been made due to 'a vigilant neighbour'. Mum decided we should keep a bit of a low profile for a while.

CHAPTER FIVE

ANIMALS AND GRAVEYARDS

Lots of this stuff I don't remember any more, at least I don't think I do. I've just heard Mum and other people talking about those times so often that sometimes I find it hard to remember which pictures and stories are really lodged in my memory and which ones are merely preserved in old photos or family anecdotes.

The first real thing I clearly remember was watching Mum being hit by her boyfriend. I don't remember the details of us living with him, or anything else about him, I just remember lying on my mattress in the corner and seeing her flying across the room. There was a lot of blood on her face.

She didn't hang around with that bloke long after that – Mum wasn't one to be a victim like the sort of battered women she sometimes met around the flats. I remember being upset by the incident, but not really frightened. I don't think I felt in any danger myself and I think I trusted Mum to be able to sort it out. I just watched it happen, like I might watch a cartoon on the telly. People are always being hit in cartoons and they just get up and keep going, which was pretty much what Mum did. I was drawing pictures of her, all covered in blood, for months afterwards.

After that Mum said that was it for her with men. 'Sod the lot of them.' From then on it was just her and me and she didn't have another boyfriend for nearly ten years. Dad got back in touch when I was six. I don't know what made him suddenly think of us, but he said he wanted to see me again, which was cool. Mum wasn't best pleased with him because she only ever got one tenner out of him for maintenance all through my childhood, even though she was having to work so hard to make ends meet, but she wanted me to be in contact with my dad if possible, so they made an arrangement for him to pick me up from the flat.

I had no memory of him but when he turned up I thought he looked really cool, with a really good image, very trendy. He didn't look like most other people's dads, which I liked. Mum was still a pretty wild punk then, still wearing the leather jackets, still changing her hair colour all the time, still looking like some Billy Idolette, but Dad had mellowed his image down a bit from the glamorous punk that Mum had first met.

Neither of us was quite sure how to handle our first father–son day out, so we went for a walk. It felt great to have a dad with me, even though he didn't feel particularly like a dad, just a big man who had turned up from nowhere.

'Let's go in there,' he suggested as we passed the gates of a graveyard.

'OK,' I agreed cheerfully. Why not? It looked like an interesting place and I didn't remember ever having been in there before, although I must have been to the graveyard with Mum when I was tiny, to return her unwanted gravestone present from Johny. We spent a wicked hour or two looking at inscriptions and reading poems about missing loved ones, about walking with the angels and all the rest. I'd learnt to read by then from studying *Garfield* cartoon books, so I could make out most of the words on my own. Mum wasn't much impressed when we got back and told her where we'd been.

'Why can't you take him bowling or to the park like a normal dad?' she wanted to know. She can't have been that surprised though, having spent so much of her own youth in punk pubs, or with goths in the Batcave. Had she forgotten that she and I had gone to the torture museum as a Christmas outing when I was really tiny? I have a feeling pretty much anything Dad could have done that day would have pissed her off.

We had to face it; none of us was that good at being normal, but I wasn't bothered. I thought it was all cool. Even then I loved people who were a bit nuts. Dad made another date to come the following week and I got myself all ready and waiting by the door in my duffel coat, wondering what we would do this time. The appointed time ticked past, the tense silence eventually shattered by the phone. It was Dad calling to tell Mum he couldn't get there because he was in bed with some other woman. I guess he was trying to punish Mum or something; there must have been a grown-up agenda going on that I knew nothing about. Not surprisingly this news really, really pissed Mum off. She said she didn't care who he was in bed with, but he shouldn't be letting me down. I cried a lot for a while, but got over it pretty quickly. There was too much interesting stuff going on in the world to worry about the bad for too long. I never liked stress, always preferring to move on and find something more cheerful to do or think about. Dad and I didn't see each other again for another ten years after that.

I loved going to stay with Nan and Grandad in the West Country. They had a garden and a paddling pool and all the things that children think are so magical, all the stuff that we couldn't have on a council estate in Peckham.

When I was about three we all went to the beach at Weymouth, with Mum's friend Virginia Astley. Virginia was a very successful singer, who Mum had met at the Guildhall at the same time as Anna Steiger. She played the flute and they sometimes used to busk together outside

Kensington tube station. Her dad had been the composer of theme tunes for Sixties television series like *The Saint* and *Danger Man*. Her elder sister had married Pete Townshend of The Who and he made a video of us at a party once, with Mum dressed as a bumblebee. Anyway, Mum and Virginia had gone off to the shops to buy something, leaving Grandad in charge of me. Seeing he was distracted rolling himself a fag, I wandered down towards the jetty, which I thought looked interesting, jutting out into the water. It was much too high for me to be able to climb up there myself, so I just held up my arms and looked pleadingly at a passing woman. She took pity and lifted me up. By the time Mum and Virginia got back I'd disappeared from sight and Grandad was a nervous wreck, certain that his negligent child-minding skills had caused the death of his grandson. They were all certain I had been abducted or drowned or something – instant paedo-alert as usual. Virginia was a bit psychic and suddenly shouted, 'I know where he is.'

She leapt up on to the jetty and ran out to the end where a group of bigger boys were jumping down twenty feet or so into the water. I was just about to take my turn, poised to launch myself off into the unknown when she got there, barged through the crowd of boys and grabbed me as I teetered on the edge. I suspect I owe her my life for that little mercy dash. Cheers, Virginia!

On a much later visit to Nan and Grandad we all went to a Sunday market in the local town. It was really interesting for me, not like anything I'd seen in South London, lots of country crafts and homemade produce. There was a stall selling live rabbits for pets. I'd had a white rabbit before, but it had escaped and disappeared and I really wanted another one to replace it.

I convinced Mum that it would be OK to keep it on the balcony of the flat and, against her better judgement, she gave in – it was hard for her to resist such a cute fluffy little thing when it was actually sitting in her hand. We bought him, christened him Buck, and took him home to London at the end of our stay. Within a couple of weeks he had doubled his size and he just kept on growing. It was like some sort of alien life form, threatening to take over the world. The balcony became a sea of poo and pee. Our family pet was a giant, furry, crapping machine. Even though Mum did everything for this ever-expanding fur-ball, cleaning up after him, shovelling food into him, he seemed to hate her with a terrible vindictiveness. She became terrified to go near him. He would stare at her malevolently and then pick up his plate in his mouth and smash it down on the floor in front of her, as if determined to show her who was boss.

When he stood on his hind legs Buck was about three feet tall and he would attack anyone who dared to come near to him apart from me, so I would hear nothing said against him. I loved him with a passion. I was sitting on the balcony cuddling him one day when something happened to make my elbow suddenly jerk and smash the patio window. It could have been an early spasm, or it could have been Buck making a sudden movement, but either way there was now a hole in the glass. Once she'd stopped tearing her hair out, Mum made a good job of patching the hole up with cardboard, but the next day, while I was at school and she was at work, Buck forced his way through the flimsy defences and into the house.

That evening when we got home the fluffy invader had made the final move in his takeover plan and we spent hours chasing him round the flat as he dived under the bed and armchairs, snarling at Mum as she struggled to flush him out. In the end she forced him out into the open, threw a sheet over him and fell on top of him, wrestling him into submission. Over the following hours we discovered that he had chewed through virtually every wire in the flat; the stereo, the iron, everything was fusing and blowing and giving off sparks as we tried to plug things in and switch them on. Mum went completely mental.

The next day, while I was at school, she felt guilty for shouting, so she went out to the local Peckham market to get another little rabbit, figuring that maybe the evil giant was just pining for company.

The moment Harry, the new rabbit, came out of his carrying box and spotted the brute of the balcony, he leapt on to his back and started rogering away like a lunatic. Like so many bullies, Buck crumpled instantly once his bluff was called. He cowered down, looking wide-eyed and terrified and just sat there taking it. It went on and on and on. Harry just never stopped, day and night, until all the hair had been ripped off Buck's back and he was shaking like a nervous wreck. The new-comer had also brought fleas into the house, which ganged up and bit Mum half to death. She decided this was my fault now, too.

We were due to go away on holiday and Mum asked a friend of mine, Zoe, to look after the rabbits while we were gone. When we got back Harry had disappeared and Zoe confessed that she had been standing up on the balcony just before we arrived, playing with him, when he had given a gigantic kick and propelled himself to free-dom over the balustrade. She and I set off to see if we could find him in the grass near the buildings, but all I managed to come up with was his head and chest, a local cat or dog having eaten the rest. Like the road kill we encountered on the way to Walsingham, this stark illus-tration of how quickly death can strike reduced me to a sobbing heap. Mum was having some people round for supper that night and she made them all swear not to mention the missing rabbit, but one of them wasn't able to keep it in – another Tourette's victim, maybe?

'So, Pete,' he said, 'what's this about a rabbit? I hear there were some remains found?'

I rushed from the table in renewed floods of tears at the tactless reminder of my bereavement.

After that Mum decided that maybe Peckham wasn't the best place to keep rabbits, so we took Buck back down to the West Country to a friend of Nan and Grandad's who had a smallholding with a pen full of rabbits. I felt very sad seeing my half-bald old friend lolloping off into the crowd, but Mum looked distinctly relieved.

Mum had got well into the Church by then, having found that one of the best ways to stop her panic attacks was to repeat the Lord's Prayer over and over again. A bit like having a tic, I suppose. She was exhausted from all the stress of her years on the road and from being a single mum, struggling to get enough money for us to live, and her religion seemed to soothe her, the Church making her feel like she belonged to a community. It suited me fine. I liked the singing and I liked watching Mum playing the violin in Frets, the clubroom behind the church hall.

Constantly on the look-out for ways to make some extra money while still being there for me, Mum got a job working for a lady called Heather, who was a high-flying Fleet Street journalist. Her job was to cook and help look after her children, AJ and Dean. She was going to be a sort of housekeeper, I suppose. It was a great gig and Heather quickly became one of our best friends, which always seemed to happen with anyone who came into Mum's life. I used to love going round to Heather's house. They had a dog called Bonzo and, even though the pit bull had tried to eat my face, I still loved dogs.

'Can we get one?' I kept nagging Mum. She kept promising that one day soon we would go to Battersea Dogs' Home and find a suitable one, but we just never seemed to get round to actually making the trip. One afternoon AJ was having a confirmation party and we were all sitting around in their house. I think Mum and Heather might have been a bit pissed on champagne; they often seemed to have a bottle on the go when they were together. I kept hearing someone tapping at the front door, but I didn't think it was my place to answer it – it wasn't my house after all.

'There's someone at the door,' I kept saying.

'Then go and answer it, for God's sake,' Heather said, irritably, obviously having had enough of children's voices for one day.

Shrugging, I made my way down the hall, but when I got there I could see through the glass that there was no shadow. It was like there was no one there. It seemed spooky and I didn't like the vibe. I hovered around for a moment, trying to pluck up my courage, but failed and went back to them to confess my failure.

'I think there's someone there, but I can't see any-one,' I explained.

'Oh, for heaven's sake,' Heather said and flounced down the hall in exasperation. She threw the door open, with me standing behind her, peering out.

A collie/Labrador dog walked straight past both of us, into the room where the party was happening, and rested its chin on Mum's lap, whimpering and staring up at her with pleading eyes. Her feet were all sore and bleeding from walking on pavements.

'Said I was going to get a dog, didn't I?' Mum said, as if it was perfectly normal for a stray dog to come knocking on a stranger's door.

Sometimes it seemed to me like my Mum had magical powers.

We called her Lassie and took her home with us at the end of the party, although we should have been able to see that she was really too much of a street dog to ever be happy cooped up in a first-floor flat. We couldn't leave her in the flat when we went round to Heather's house to work because she would crap on the carpets and chew the furniture, so the next day we took her with us. Bonzo jumped on her the moment she arrived, just like the horny little rabbit. I could see them stuck together in the garden and immediately had a feeling things had got serious. We tried turning the hose on them, but nothing worked and a few weeks later we had eight puppies in the flat. There was one honey-coloured one, four black ones and three browns and they all yapped like seagulls whenever Lassie escaped through the window and left them on their own, which seemed to happen most days, driving the neighbours into a frenzy of annoyance.

I thought the whole pet thing was really cool – the more the merrier as far as I was concerned – but Mum had just bought herself her first fitted carpets ever and Lassie was crapping all over them whenever the urge took her. As if that wasn't enough, there was some sort of back surge in the plumbing system in the flats at the same time and everyone else's sewage came roaring up into our toilet and overflowed over the rim, like some sort of horror scene from *Trainspotting*. We were back to bare boards and for a while Mum thought the Devil might be coming after her again.

Eventually it was obvious we couldn't keep Lassie any more, although Heather gave a home to the honey-coloured puppy, which lived to a great age and finally passed away while I was in the *Big Brother* house. I was heartbroken to see Lassie go because I really loved her. Someone came in a car to take her away. She jumped in through the back door, all excited about this new adventure, and as the car drove off she gazed out the back window at me as if she was waving goodbye. It was horrible.

After that we just had cats.

Nan and Grandad had a black mongrel called Buster who I used to draw all the time. Grandad knew a bit about art and he was always telling everyone how brilliant my pictures were. Buster was a good friend to me and one night I had a vision about him. In the vision we were staying at Nan and Grandad's house and Buster was beckoning me to the end of the garden because he wanted to say goodbye. He turned round, gave me one last look and then disappeared into a golden light, a bit like the light that had surrounded the Angel Michael. I knew immediately he was dead and told Mum. The next day my aunt rang to tell Mum that Buster had been put down because the vet had said his bones were starting to snap with age. We worked out that the vet must have been doing the deed at the same moment I had the vision.

Having visions like this frightened me sometimes. At the same time it was also pretty cool to be able to see little glimpses of the future, as if I had a few magical powers myself, an in-built crystal ball.

DAVE

Even though Mum had lots of men friends, not all of them were raving poofs; they were mostly colleagues, street performers and fellow musicians. She didn't get another actual boyfriend though until Dave came along. She met him in the Peckham Tenants' Hall where he was part of a party. She had gone into the hall to get a coke for me and my friend, Zoe. She only had a pound on her and so she couldn't afford anything for herself, or even any crisps for us. The party was in full swing and no one seemed to mind us crashing it. Everyone was very friendly and welcoming. There was a big fat strip-o-gram doing her thing, which was really funny and not even remotely sexy, so Mum didn't mind us watching. Mum got chatting to this tall guy at the bar who had all this long dark hair. He was dressed up as a woman, with a pair of plastic tits.

'Got your true colours on tonight then, have you, love?' Mum teased.

'Yeah,' he said. 'Don't tell anyone.'

They both burst out laughing and got chatting while Mum bought our cokes.

'I've never asked a bloke to buy me a drink before in my life,' Mum said, 'but would you buy me a half of lager and I'll pay you back one day? I can give you a song I've recorded if you like.'

He obviously liked her style because he bought her the drink and accepted the tape she had in her bag as payment. He seemed really excited about the transaction, saying he couldn't wait to listen to it. It seemed he had an interest in music too. What Mum hadn't realized was that she had written her telephone number on the cassette box – probably in case it fell into the hands of a record producer and he wanted to offer her millions of pounds to sign to his label. She had started to feel better about her life by then and had gone back to playing and writing a bit of music. Anyway, this bloke with the plastic tits, Dave, got in touch a few days later, having listened to the tape and decided he liked what he heard. He then went to see Mum in a concert at Covent Garden, and he started coming round to the flat once a week on his motorbike, just to hang out with us.

He was wicked, really into his music. He had a studio in the garage where he lived and let me use it without ever making a fuss or worrying I might break anything. Totally cool. I called him Dad from the first day he came to visit, which made Mum a bit nervous, but he didn't seem to care. He actually seemed to quite like it; nothing much seemed to bother Dave.

As well as getting her music together again, Mum was also trying to do something with her art, which she felt she had been neglecting for too long. She had been making some enquiries and had been accepted as a mature student on an art course at Brighton University. She was really keen to go down there to study. Her dad had insisted she give up art so she could concentrate on her music when she was at school and she had always regretted it. She was so happy to be accepted and we moved out of Peckham and down to Brighton for a year – living by the seaside! Brilliant!

Mum enjoyed the course, but it was hard for her to hang out with the other students, most of whom were just out of school, when she had already lived a colourful life, travelling the world with famous pop groups, having me, and all those experiences that change you and make it hard to go back to thinking the same way you thought when you first set out on adult life. I would go to school during the day and then would often go round to the university to wait for her to finish her classes. I liked it there because the people Mum knew in the music department used to let me play around in the sound studios and would show me how everything worked. I was never afraid to ask questions or to show an interest, and adults always responded well to that. It would have been difficult to have been shy in the life we led, with so many different people coming and going all the time.

Dave used to ride down from London at weekends on his bike to visit. When he asked Mum to marry him, and told her his mother had offered to lend him some money for a deposit on a house, Mum decided it was time to give up the student life and get on with being a grown-up. So she accepted his proposal and we headed back to South London. Married! Dave was going to be my actual dad, it was perfect, couldn't have been better.

Taking on a new dad meant I also got to take on a whole new family, including a new set of grand-parents. Dave's mum and dad, my new grandparents-to-be, were a bit of an entertainment all on their own. I had never seen anything like them before. Richard, his dad, hadn't spoken for six years, apart from muttering 'Bootsie, Bootsie' at the cat all day long. He used to clomp back and forth through the house, nailing open the back door and then the front door to get a gale blowing through the rooms. Alice, Dave's mum, was the maddest Irish woman ever, always talking in sayings.

'Bad company'll lead yer to the gallows,' she'd announce out of the blue, leaving us all struggling for a suitable response and trying to suppress our giggles.

She found out Mum had some Romany blood in her and from then on referred to her as 'the filthy feckin' tinker'. I always liked the idea of being descended from gypsies; it seemed glamorous and romantic. I pictured them in painted caravans, living on the open road, breaking in wild horses, wearing gold earrings and brightly coloured headscarves, sitting round the camp fires recounting folk tales into the small hours of the night. It conjured up a hundred different images. It was my great granddad, Nan's dad, who had been the real Romany, working as a rag-and-bone man and living on a campsite somewhere in Mitcham. Mum used to be able to speak a bit of their language when she was young and Nan still remembers a lot of the folklore of her youth. But none of these romantic images were coming to Alice's mind when she thought of 'filthy feckin' tinkers'.

Richard would plod out into the garden occasionally with a large pair of scissors and snip all the buds off the rose bushes, just as they were about to open, like a character from *Alice in Wonderland*. There was a big vine covered in grapes growing up the wall, until he just took an axe to it for no reason one day. It was all mad, but endlessly funny to a small boy hungry for eccentricity. Alice used to buy potatoes by the ton and be boiling up urns of soup all the time, but it always used to have things like chicken's feet floating in it and I would get uncontrollable giggles whenever I was confronted by a bowl of the stuff.

All the time she was preparing a meal she would be muttering to herself as she gathered up the ingredients: 'We'll boil the hell out o' that! And we'll boil the feck out o' that!'

I would spend hours drawing cartoons of her because she fascinated me so much, with a cigarette permanently glued to her lips, always spitting and sneezing into the food and then, when accused, swearing blind she hadn't, filled with indignation at the very suggestion. I eventually managed to animate the cartoons on Photoshop, turning the adventures of Alice into a little home movie.

At Christmas she would find an old plastic toy, discarded from a McDonald's Happy Meal in the distant past, which had been gathering grime in the corner of a cupboard somewhere ever since, and would wrap it up as my Christmas present. She would take her teeth out at the end of a meal, swish them clean in her teacup, put them back in and then drink down the contents of the cup. I would watch every move with fascinated, open-mouthed horror.

'What the feck are you laffing at?' she would demand whenever she caught me laughing and, when I couldn't answer with a straight face, she would push her finger into my face. 'Laff at that!'

Alice, however, for all her madness, was the first person to see I had developed some funny little twitches. They had crept up so slowly and gradually that Mum and I hadn't even noticed them. They were just what I did, part of who I was.

'Look at yer!' Alice would snap. 'What's all this?'

She would do an imitation of me and Mum would become indignant, thinking she was picking on me, particularly when she described me as 'the Divil's child'. I didn't like that suggestion at all, but the Devil played a large part in Alice's life. She had all these statues of Jesus and Mary on the walls and every so often she would get them down on the floor and start wailing about how she wasn't a prostitute, even though nobody had ever suggested that she was – it was wild, like visiting the set of *Father Ted* for real.

I felt that having Dave as a dad was going to bring all sorts of extra entertainment my way.

CHAPTER SEVEN

WARNING SIGNS

We had a couple of friends called Lizzie-Anne and Kaye. Lizzie-Anne was in the process of changing from being Alan. It seemed a bit wild to be changing sex in order to have a lesbian relationship, but variety always makes life a bit more interesting. They were lovely people and they used to look after me sometimes when Mum had stuff to do. We met them through Poofy-Cousin-Marcus, who had known Alan when he was a man, and actually believed he might have been the reason Alan got a bit confused about his sexuality in the first place, finding him wandering about the house in women's shoes after their first night together. Lizzie-Anne was working as an usherette at the Palace Theatre and got us free tickets to go and see *Starlight Express* – great show, I thought, but a crap storyline! A theatre critic already and hardly even out of short pants!

After I'd been staying with Lizzie-Anne and Kaye one time they spotted something funny about me and asked Mum if she'd ever noticed that I seemed to have little absences, where I would just drift away from the world and not seem to hear or see anything for a few minutes, almost like I'd gone to sleep with my eyes open but the lids drooping. I think the official name for such attacks is 'petit mals' and they are little seizures. I hadn't realized I was doing anything odd, just thought I was a bit of a daydreamer I suppose, because I still liked to live inside my head much of the time.

Apparently they'd woken up in the night to find me standing bolt upright at the bedroom door, being a bit strange, like Damien in *The Omen* – 'Pete the Anti-Christ'. Anyway, whatever they told Mum got her thinking a bit and she decided to take me to the doctor just to check there wasn't anything she should be worrying about. The doctor didn't seem to have much idea what was going on either and suggested it might be some mild form of childhood epilepsy that I would grow out of in time. I felt fine, so I wasn't worried, perfectly happy to have 'little absences' now and then.

I had a thing about the parting in my hair at that time. The line had to be exactly and perfectly razor straight before I felt I could safely leave the house. People used to call me 'Peter Parting' because it became such an obsession. It was just the tiniest warning rumble of the storm that was soon to come, so quiet and small that nobody, including me, took much notice. These things were just part of being Pete. Now and then a faint suspicion would flit across my mind that there might be something different about me, but I wouldn't have had a clue how to explain it to anyone, or ask for help, and none of it gave me any problem, so why worry? If the doctor and Mum weren't worried, then there was nothing to concern me, was there?

I was about nine when Mum got pregnant. I liked the idea of having a baby brother or sister, especially with Dave there to be our dad. I was always going on to Mum about getting one, as if you could buy them in the same markets as the baby rabbits.

When she had Alex it was great. I had my own baby brother and I instantly loved him to death. We had become a proper family unit, Mum, Dad and two kids, like something from the television ads.

I didn't have any trouble getting friends at that stage, particularly girls. I had a best friend from school called Sarah and we used to spend hours making tapes for our own radio station. It was our version of Capital Radio, which we listened to a lot, and we called it 'Completely and Utterly Ballsed Up Piece of Birds' Droppings, Mixed up in Beaver Sweat Sauce and Totally Crappy and Unorganized Big Turd Radio' – catchy eh? It was a great jingle. We would record all the links and interviews and make up our own songs on the spot on a Casio keyboard or any instruments we could find, even though neither of us could play any of them properly.

I was the host of the show, and most of the guests as

well. I would use different voices to interview myself, then I would use two tape recorders together to over-dub myself over and over again, so there would be a great big group of me to interview, hundreds of mad voices all interrupting and talking over one another, a bit like they did inside my head most of the time. I think I imagined I would work in the music business when I grew up, maybe as a producer or something.

I wanted to spend as much time as I could fiddling about in the studio and to create a whole album of my own songs. I didn't have any particular musical taste at the time. I mostly just liked whatever group Mum was playing with and whatever music I was exposed to as a result. I had a period where I was really into The Prodigy, who had come out of the underground rave scene and also did hard-core techno at the time. Their song 'Smack My Bitch Up' had caused a bit of controversy. But I could just as easily trip out to pre-packaged stuff like the Spice Girls. I was open to anything, having been brought up on all the different sorts of music Mum was involved in. I was in the choir at school and I could hold a tune, although to be honest I had a bit of a shit voice.

As well as the radio station, I was also creating my own world in cartoon form, making up the sort of stories you would normally find in magazines like *Viz*, which I read avidly. Mum grumbled that I was obsessed with turds and poo, but aren't all small boys? I was always writing poems about things like that, and drawing little cartoon illustrations of talking turds with flies buzzing around their heads.

'Why can't you write poems about nice things?' Mum would complain, but that just made me laugh. Where would be the fun in that? Turds were hysterical, weren't they?

She might have tutted and said grown-up things like that from time to time, but Mum still liked to sit and watch *Beavis and Butt-head* with me and I often caught her laughing at the jokes. I thought those two guys were so cool. The jokes were so good, and the words like Assmunch, buttwipe, penis breath, schlong, dil-hole, dil-weed, asswipe and butt dumpling brought me endless hours of sniggering happiness. *Ren and Stimpy*, the cat and the Chihuahua with a fiery temper, brought me the same kind of joy. Their writers seemed to see life from a whole new perspective, catching me by surprise but at the same time saying things that summed up exactly how I felt about things.

Big laughs come from the unexpected; the unexpected prat fall or unexpected slant on something familiar. I think that is why I am sometimes able to make people laugh, because I take them by surprise. Half the time I take myself by surprise with the things that plop out of my mouth, or the positions my body arbitrarily falls into. I loved to laugh and I loved to make other people laugh. I wanted to be as funny as Beavis and Butt-head, I wanted to draw them and write for them and be them. I wanted to be a genius like their creator, Mike Judge.

The feature film that obsessed me the most was *Alien*; everything about it, from the soundtrack to Sigourney Weaver, from the model making to the plot, was faultless. The *Alien* films are the perfect thrillers and one of the first things I bought myself when I came out of the *Big Brother* house with a bit of money was a model of the Alien's head. It's like a collector's thing in a glass case. Really cool.

Sometimes I had a suspicion I could sense some sort of alien living inside me and I worried that one day it would come bursting out of my chest, just like I'd seen it come out of John Hurt's, and reveal itself in all its grinning horror before scuttling off into a dark hidden corner to plot its next move. As it turned out, my suspicions weren't so far from the truth; the alien's eggs were hatching somewhere deep inside my nervous system, preparing themselves for the battle to come.

CHAPTER EIGHT

A FAMILY UNIT

Dave and Mum got married and it was a great wedding. Mum had seventeen bridesmaids and I was the only pageboy. With my incredibly straight parting and my even straighter suit and tie I looked more like Macaulay Culkin than the offspring of a couple of hippy-punks. We may have looked like a surprisingly straight family for the day, but some of the congregation still looked more *Rocky Horror Show* than *Little House on the Prairie*. Half of them were poofs because Mum knew so many. Poofy-Cousin-Marcus, Lizzie-Anne and Kaye all came dressed in black, like three crows in a row, silently registering their disapproval at the cuteness of the whole proceedings. Maybe they all thought Mum was selling out to the straight world by having a traditional wedding and putting Dave and me in suits and ties for the day. Even Alex was wearing a little collar and tie. I thought it was fun because it was so different to how things normally were around us; it was like playing a part.

Nan and Grandad had to leave half way through the afternoon because Grandad had to get back to his local pub before opening time. He was always a stickler for his routines. Maybe he was a bit obsessional too! Wow! So many possibilities for weird behaviour in my gene pool, so much rogue DNA swirling around, looking for a place to settle.

At the reception after the ceremony Dave took care of all the music and he and I planned a surprise number for me to perform as a wedding present to Mum. I slipped away to another room, my heart thumping with excitement, and changed out of my wedding suit and into a pair of Mum's multicoloured skin-tight leggings and a psychedelic top. I then greased back my hair and stuck on a moustache. Tonight, ladies and gentlemen, I was going to be Freddy Mercury, miming to 'Bohemian Rhapsody'. I loved Freddy and I loved getting up and giving a performance in front of an audience. I'd done a Freddy impression once in a school concert and knew it went down well with people. The moment I walked out into the spotlight I felt instantly comfortable on the stage in front of everyone, feeling their eyes on me, seeing their smiles as I started my act, and afterwards hearing them clap and tell me how brilliant I'd been. Some people would rather die than be the centre of attention, standing in the spotlight, other people just know it's the right place for them. To me, it felt completely right.

Soon after they got married, Dave bought us an old Victorian family house just round the corner from where we had been living in Plumstead. It had been owned by an old lady who hadn't done anything to it for years. There was one room that was particularly gloomy and depressing, and that was designated to be my bedroom. I kept telling Mum the room was evil, that there was something awful in the vibes, but I could tell she wasn't taking me seriously. I felt that things moved around it in the dead of night and shapes would appear in front of me, which I was sure were ghosts or demons or poltergeists.

'Don't be so silly,' Mum would say, assuming I was just making up excuses not to go to bed. 'You've got to go to sleep now.'

In the end she agreed to come and sleep in there with me, just to prove there was nothing to be scared of. That night she climbed into bed and turned the light out. I waited quietly to see what would happen next. I could tell she was nervous despite her protestations, and wasn't dropping off to sleep. There was a lot of sighing and thumping about in the bed as she tried to get comfortable. Then she turned the light back on again. She'd left a glass of water on the dressing table a little way across the room and it suddenly shattered, spraying shards of glass and water everywhere. Mum let out a blood-curdling scream, grabbed me and we ran back to bed with Dave. None of us went back in that room for as long as we lived in that house.

* * *

Having a baby brother was great because it gave me a permanent audience and Alex was always very appreciative of any show I liked to put on for him. I made a set of finger puppets out of felt and then wrote full-scale musicals for them to perform. I could operate all ten of my fingers simultaneously as different characters. There was a crocodile, a policeman, a dog, a robot and banana-man. It was like a mini finger *Muppet Show*. Mum had bought us an old piano and I would use that to build the musicals, taping the songs to intersperse with the dialogue. I don't know how much of it Alex took in; he probably just liked having his big brother's attention and watching the bright colours of the felt, but it seemed like he was enthusiastic as he gurgled and clapped, laughed and drooled his appreciation. One day, once he was moving about more, he shut his finger in the piano by accident and it all went horribly septic, so I invented a character called 'Big Green Scary Finger'.

As he got older and started toddling around the house I noticed that Mum was forever having to stop him from injuring himself on household items. I could hear her continually saying, 'Don't touch that, Alex,' 'Put that down, Alex,' 'Don't do that, Alex, it's dangerous.' I'd just been given a Sega Megadrive and so I designed a game called 'Alex the Palix' (which was Mum's nickname for him). On the first level of the game he had to overcome a load of dangerous household obstacles like 'Terror the Toaster' and 'Miserable Matches'; another character was a predatory bottle of bleach and another was a kettle that could pour boiling water over you if you touched the flex. If a player got to the second level they would move on to nursery school and face new dangers and then on to main school where they would fight the bullies, and finally to the fourth level where the enemy would be teenage gangs with flick knives. It was all done to the Tetris music and I used all my own fears and experiences to colour it. I dreamt that maybe one day I could sell the game to Sega and make a fortune, so we would never have any more money worries and Mum could live in the sort of house she always dreamt about, with a garden and trees, and she wouldn't have to keep going on at Dave about earning a living.

I was eleven when I moved on to my secondary school. There was a girl there who was really pretty and I fell seriously in love for the first time. I always got on better with girls than boys – a bit girlie from the start, I guess, not keen on playing football or any of the other boyish stuff. I had started to be teased by the tough boys at my last school and I never wanted to fight back, which made me even more of a tempting target. I did try to stick up for myself a few times, but I couldn't do it properly, so then I would get beaten up even more for daring to even assume I could answer back. The tics and twitches that Alice had noticed, and the strangeness that Lizzie-Anne and Kaye had remarked on, must have been becoming more apparent to the outside world, because the other boys were picking up on it. They could also tell I was a bit soft, always a cardinal sin among boys. Hard is what's cool.

Despite my oddness this girl agreed to become my girlfriend, but then she started behaving very oddly, giving me a hard time, and she got a bit funny when I asked her what the matter was. To start with she denied there was anything wrong, then she told me her dad was having it off with her. I was stunned. I might have been surrounded by a lot of weirdos in my life, but I had never had anyone even try to do something unpleasant to me in that way. The thought of it lodged itself deep in my imagination. I started to get really unsettled. Mum could see there was something wrong and made me tell her what was worrying me. When I eventually spat it out she went straight up to the school to talk to the headmaster – why do mothers always have to do that, even when you beg them not to? He basically told her to sort it out with my girlfriend's mother, which didn't seem quite appropriate. In the end I rang Childline myself and told them what was going on. They investigated but it turned out she was making it up just to seem more interesting to me, or something – and I thought I was weird! I decided I had moved out of my depth emotionally and didn't get another girlfriend after that for a few years.

Even though I could think of a million other things I would rather have been doing with my time, I did have to play football now and then. I suppose the school had to make sure we took some exercise and did some sport. They put me in goal and I was actually quite good at it; I guess I had quick reflexes, part of the general condition that was starting to bubble up inside me. I was happy to throw myself around with very little fear, which meant I made some spectacular saves.

The trouble was I utterly dreaded letting in any goals because then everyone on the team would get cross and shout at me. I hated letting the other team members down. I still find it very hard to disappoint people, even when I know there's nothing I can do about it and it really isn't my fault. I suppose I just want to be loved unconditionally all the time. That certainly wasn't happening. In fact it was becoming more like the opposite. More and more people around the school seemed to be starting to hate me, particularly the boys. They began calling me names like 'monkey-face'. They said it so often I was convinced it must be true, that I actually did have a face like a monkey.

'It's not personal, for goodness sake,' Mum would tell me as she watched from behind the goal as I got upset at some insult shouted at me. 'It's just part of the sport. You're doing brilliantly, just keep concentrating on the game.'

I could see what she meant, but I still didn't like upsetting people and longed to be allowed to give the game up for good so there was no more danger of letting goals in. Mum was always very good when I told her about being bullied at school. Most of the time, however, I kept it to myself, knowing that she would immediately want to go up to see the teachers and tell them what was going on, which I knew would have bad consequences for me. Whenever she did intervene for me, the teachers never seemed to believe her anyway.

I did still have one or two friends who remained loyal for as long as they could, but I guess it was growing increasingly difficult for them as I became more of a figure of fun. Boys always want to be seen with the cool guys; no one wanted to be the poor sad sod who had to hang out with 'monkey-face'.

The worst betrayal came when my last best mate announced to the whole world that I was gay. He made up a story about how I'd grabbed his balls in the shower and started playing with his willy. Later I found out he did it because he wanted to put my girlfriend off me so that another of his mates could go out with her. Maybe that was true, but I think he had also decided to put some distance between us for the sake of his own reputation. A bit of a Judas really, but I can understand now how much pressure he must have been under.

No one seemed to find it hard to believe that I might be gay, except me – and nothing much has changed since then either. I'd known enough poofs in my life to be able to understand what the job required and I knew I didn't fulfil the necessary criteria. But I did

know I was a bit girly, and I was not particularly bothered about hiding it. Well, I wasn't able to hide it really.
I could hardly butch up overnight. And that was all the
evidence the playground jury needed to convict me. The
whole school started saying it, chanting insults after me
wherever I went. Statistically speaking, there must have
been some real gays in the school somewhere, but none
of them wanted to stick their heads above the parapet
and come to my defence. I was on my own.

There was one boy in particular who had it in for
me, peeing all over me in the toilets and picking on me
all the time, particularly when he could get together an
audience. When I told Mum about this bloke and how
unhappy he was making me she went ape and stormed
up to the school to complain again, but they just told
her this other boy had problems of his own and they
didn't seem to think they should do anything about it.
They suggested perhaps I should see a child psychologist,
as I always seemed to prefer being with the girls in the
playground to the boys. That sent Mum completely
mental. I needed psychiatric help because I preferred
playing with girls? If that's the case there must be an
awful lot of nutters out there on the loose in the world.
He likes hanging out with women? Lock him up and
throw away the key!

I wasn't just unpopular with the boys; the teachers
were also beginning to complain to Mum that I was messing about and not concentrating in class. They thought I

was acting strange and clowning around, but I wasn't really aware of it. I'd been trying to keep a low profile rather than attracting attention to myself. They said I was squinting a lot and I was aware of that, not realizing it was a crime. I kept doing it to try to get rid of a sort of phantom ache that would appear behind my eyes every few minutes.

As well as squinting I was starting to shake my head, a bit like a dog with something stuck in its ear, trying to clear an annoying tingle. Mum wondered if I needed my eyes tested but I thought it was more to do with being upset about this girlfriend – ex-girlfriend now – and the bullyboys. Just in case, Mum took me to the hospital and they decided to give me a brain scan. I don't know what they thought they might see, but at the end they said they couldn't find anything wrong. If there was an alien in there it was fucking clever at hiding itself.

I was becoming increasingly sure there was something going wrong inside my head, but I couldn't work out how to explain it to anyone. Not knowing what else to do I just kept soldiering on, hoping it would right itself eventually, but it was growing worse all the time.

One teacher called Mum up to the school to tell her I now had an attitude problem. I'd been late getting into school a few days before and when that happened you had to fill in a reason in the book, so that morning I had written, 'Got up far too late, man,' which was an entirely

truthful reason. According to the teacher who had sum-
moned us, this was a sexist comment and I should have
written 'man/woman' or something. She also thought it
was disrespectful to her, which I guess was true. Mum
tried to explain that Dave was a bit of an old hippie and
I had probably picked up the word 'man' from him, but
she was sure I was just as likely to use it to address a
girl as a boy. One minute they were worried because I
preferred being with the girls to the boys; the next they
were telling me off for being sexist.

The stupidity of this confrontation was the final
straw for Mum. She hadn't liked the way the teachers
were dealing with me for some time, so she decided to
move me to another school, called Waterfield. She'd been
doing some adult education classes there herself and
thought it looked like a nice place. I certainly wasn't
going to argue.

Things smoothed out for a bit at Waterfield. I
stopped feeling the need to blink the whole time and
began to feel comfortable. I loved the school and wanted
to please the teachers. Good move! I was getting As and
Bs and the whole 'model pupil' thing. Maybe, I thought,
I had been worrying unnecessarily; maybe there was
nothing wrong with me after all. Maybe I had just been a
square peg in a round hole at the last school, or whatever the saying is.

A few of the Waterfield tough guys picked on me at
first, just like at the previous school, but for some reason

they seemed to warm to me once they got to know me. They seemed to like me because I was odd, adopting me as their token weird guy rather than punishing me for being who I was. I began to think that maybe life didn't have to be so bad after all. The art classes were great and I started to do dance as well, which I found I had a real flair for. I loved it. I became a bit of a boffin in class, ending up with the most merit points in the whole school. I even became a teachers' pet, all very different from what had been developing before.

When the teachers decided to do *Aladdin* as the school play I was cast as the genie from the lamp, playing the part the same way that Robin Williams had done it in the Disney film, with all the different voices rushing over one another, a kaleidoscope of characters and jokes. I knew I would be able to do it. I could do the talking fast act standing on my head, and I was always being different characters when I was playing with Sarah or other friends, complete with all the Robin Williams-type noises and the energy. As I've said, Mum told me that Dad used to be the same – another character trait that must have come from the DNA, man!

When I went to the auditions for the play everyone else was singing 'A Whole New World', the sweet song from the movie, but I wanted to do something a bit different, wanted to stand out, make an impact, so I sang 'Look for the bare necessities, the simple bare necessities' from *Jungle Book*. Everyone laughed like I'd hoped they would and gave me the part. It's such a great feeling when you make people laugh, make them happy.

The audience loved my performance and it felt so good to be able to control their reactions, feel their encouragement, feel them wanting more. It gave me a buzz to know I could do something so well. I knew Mum was really proud, and a bit surprised too maybe. I'd played Pharaoh in *Joseph and His Amazing Technicolor Dreamcoat* at the previous school but the part hadn't exactly given me the same scope to show what I could do. This was more my moment to shine, just as *Big Brother* would be ten years later. The genie was more like how I was in real life. Because the teachers all seemed to like me at Waterfield they all supported me, encouraged me, told me that I could achieve great things if I wanted to. That was nice stuff to hear, exciting, something to look forward to. Life was becoming sweet again, but it wasn't going to stay that way for long. This was the final calm before the great storm.

CHAPTER NINE

THE EXPLOSION

Dave was beginning to get on Mum's nerves but I still really liked him. He was always great to me. He was my dad and that was how he always acted. But Mum said he just got pissed all day and didn't do anything to help her earn a living or look after Alex and me. He'd given up the job as a maintenance man at the Freemasons' Hall in Covent Garden which he'd had when they got married, and just wanted to make music all day in his studio – which I could totally understand because I loved being in there with him. He was like a really great mate as well as a dad.

The studio looked like the control module of a spaceship and Dave seemed to be able to do anything he wanted in there. He would record my voice, sample it and turn it into a track in minutes. It was like magic! He and Mum would write music and record a lot together, too, in the evenings, and I loved just being there with them, watching and listening, learning all the time. He was a fantastic sound engineer and used to get a brilliant sound out of everything.

It was him who bought me the Sega Megadrive for Christmas, the one that inspired me to write the Alex the Palix game. It was the most wicked present anyone had ever given me. It made me cry when I unwrapped it because I was so happy. When I was in the *Big Brother* house Nikki asked if I had ever had anything make me cry with happiness, and I could still recall that Christmas Day, even ten years afterwards. I don't think that was the sort of answer Nikki had been looking for, but what can you do? You've got to tell it like it is.

The studio seemed like a natural habitat to me. I'd always found computers easy to understand – I never had to bother with reading manuals or anything like that, just followed my instincts and experimented until I got the result I wanted.

But Dave and his mates and me having a happy time in the studio wasn't helping Mum to put food on the table and she was becoming increasingly frustrated. Being the only professional musician in the house and having played on God knows how many number one records, to be constantly sent to make the tea by Dave and his mates while they concentrated on doing great creative things was beginning to get her down. She finally decided she'd had enough and announced that we were going. That meant her, me and Alex, heading off back into the world without a dad again to try to cope on our own.

'It's not that I don't still love Dave,' she explained to me. 'It's just that it's all too much hard work. It's like looking after twenty kids instead of two.'

It was absolutely miserable to think we wouldn't be living with Dave any more but it wasn't really my business, and I could understand why Mum was fed up with doing all the work and being the only proper grown-up in the family. If I'd had magical powers I would have made it different. I would have got Dave a job so he could have made Mum happy.

I guess Alex was too small to really know what was going on but I was sorry for him too, not to be living with his dad any more, because I already knew what that felt like. I cried for ages, but I didn't try to change Mum's mind. It was grown-up business. I didn't know what had really gone on between them and I didn't want to ask. All I knew was that he had been the only dad I'd really known, he'd always been kind to me and he'd taught me a lot of good stuff in the studio. I learnt how to make music from him and losing him felt like bollocks.

I haven't seen him much since the day Mum packed us up and we left, although Alex has. He lives in Germany now and Alex was over there staying with him when I was in the *Big Brother* house. I had dreams about him for a long time and I know he had dreams about me too because eventually he got in touch and told me about them.

Anyway, we were a threesome now, and Mum got us re-housed in a council flat in Greenwich. Greenwich, for those who don't know it, is a beautiful historic part of London, lying beside the River Thames and is home to the *Cutty Sark*, one of London's biggest and most beautiful tourist attractions. As a result the area is full of tourists and rich, trendy people who work across the river in the City and can afford to pay high house prices in exchange for great views. But that is only half the story. If one of those tourists turned round a few wrong corners he would find himself emerging into a different landscape, the concrete jungle where our new home was, a jungle made up of hideous multi-storey blocks glowering over dangerous, ugly communal wastelands.

The flat we had been allocated was beautiful inside, more like a full-sized house, with a giant window on one side looking out over Greenwich Park, while on the other side we could see the dome of St Paul's Cathedral and the river. But the walls were thin as paper and we could hear every harsh sound that went on around us. Discarded sofas smoked in the stairwells after being ignited by the gangs of teenagers who lurked in every corner, waiting to jump out at anyone who left themselves vulnerable. They lounged on the stairways, outside the local shops and round the lifts, constantly looking for someone to give them an excuse for a fight or a quick fix of excitement.

I might have been able to convince myself that they were all swagger and no substance, but almost in the first week we were there I saw a lone man brought down to the ground by a group of them as they stripped him of his wallet and anything else of value. It was like watching a pack of hyenas closing in on an antelope that had inadvertently got itself separated from the herd.

From that moment I was petrified to even walk outside the flat. Just getting to the school bus was a scary nightmare, every movement and sound making me jump in anticipation of an attack. I was always hurrying everywhere, my eyes averted, terrified of being noticed, terrified of rounding a corner and coming face-to-face with the enemy. In most cases I never even knew who they were, they were just anonymous, threatening figures on the horizon, but they seemed to know who I was. The moment they spotted me they would immediately go into action, shouting abuse, threatening to beat me up, and I would feel my legs turning to jelly as I tried to escape without tempting them to give chase.

We had a maisonette on the top two floors, but getting to it was a heart-stopping obstacle course. The lifts in the block were always splattered with urine, vomit and dog turds, the walls covered with globs of phlegm, so you didn't want to touch them or lean against them. The staircases held a fear of the unknown at every corner and turning. One morning we came out of the flat to find someone had wanked off on our letterbox. When she first saw it Mum thought it was egg whites.

It was like living in a world full of aliens that I didn't know or understand and could only fear. I would try to stay indoors as much as possible but sometimes I had to go out to the shops for something and I was terrified every step of the way. I dreamt of moving to the safety of the country, but I knew there was no chance of that. I knew from visiting Nan and Grandad in the West Country how safe and nice it felt there.

At least I was safe when I was at school, and happy with the way things were going. But then another blow fell, taking away even these few hours of security a day. The school announced it was failing to attract enough pupils and was being forced to close down. I was going to have to go somewhere else, somewhere that for all I knew might easily be filled with strangers like the ones who lurked round every corner of the estate.

I was informed that I was to attend Thomas Tallis School in Eltham, which was supposed to be the best school in the area but which I knew nothing about. It had taken me so much time and effort to win over everyone at Waterfield and now I was going to have to go through the whole process again. What if I didn't pull it off this time? What if they turned on me like they had at the school before Waterfield? What if they hated me and hunted me down and beat me? The anxiety was like a vice gripping the inside of my head, making me feel like it was about to burst.

When I arrived at Thomas Tallis on the first morning

and went to the classroom I'd been allocated to I felt a glimmer of optimism. This wasn't as bad as I'd feared. Everyone seemed very nice, quite comfortable, not threatening at all. Maybe this wasn't going to be a problem. I breathed a sigh of relief as I settled in behind my desk. Maybe I would be able to get away with this move after all. The teacher started to take our names.

'Oh, sorry,' he said when he got to me, 'you should be in the other class.'

Feeling the anxiety returning I crossed to the correct classroom, already feeling exposed and vulnerable. Maybe this one would be as pleasant as the last, I told myself. No need to worry, surely. But the moment I walked into this new room every head turned towards me and it wasn't a good feeling. There was no welcome to be had here. Every pair of eyes looked hostile. These guys did not want me in their class. I was an outsider, an intruder, and not like them. They had already decided they didn't like me and they had already decided I was gay because I didn't have a crew cut like every other boy in the room, and like most of the other boys in the school.

I kept my head down and stayed as quiet as my nervous twitching would allow. When the second lesson started another boy swaggered in and stared at me.

'Why that boy in my chair?' he demanded to know.

Again I felt every pair of eyes in the room turn on to me as I tried to shrink away to nothing.

The pattern was the same as before, although this time the names were different.

'Hey, Mop-head!' they would shout.

'Hey, camel! Camel-camel-camel!'

Camel? Monkey? It seemed I was turning into an entire fucking zoo. Why couldn't I just be Pete?

Waterfield School had been a sanctuary from the threatening atmosphere of the estate, but here aggression and violence were the norm, just as they were around the flat, and from that moment on my life became a nightmare with no respite anywhere apart from behind our spunk-splattered front door.

All I wanted was to be invisible so they wouldn't notice me, but it seemed that my body had other ideas. It seemed to be determined to get me noticed, and not in a good way. I knew I had a few funny little habits by then, but that was just the way I was, nothing I could do about it most of the time. I knew I was beginning to twitch involuntarily a bit in class, which got on the other boys' nerves. I would try to hold the twitches in, but occasionally they would get beyond my control and splutter out, always when I was close to someone who was likely to react badly, when the pressure to hold them in was the greatest. Pressure wasn't good. Pressure made me want to explode. I didn't handle pressure well.

'Why you doing that in my face, boy?'

'What's wrong with you, man? What's wrong with you?'

I didn't know the answer to that. I couldn't explain what was happening. The bullies, with their loud, indignant, mocking voices, soon made sure everyone else had noticed what was happening too.

If I was frightened by what was going on in the physical environment around me, I was even more frightened by the weird things that seemed to be starting to happen deep inside my brain and my body. It was no longer just the little twitches and tics that Dave's mum, Alice, had noticed any more, these were things that no one could overlook. It seemed she had been right, maybe I was the 'Divil's Child', or maybe I had been right and there was an alien living inside me, taking over my body piece by piece, eating into my brain, taking control, making me do things I didn't want to do, operating me like some badly coordinated string puppet – 'Pinocchio Pete'. It sounds mad to even suggest such things, but what was happening to me was mad, unreal, not like anything I had ever had experience of, or heard about. I didn't know anyone else who was having these problems. I had no one to study or compare myself to. Everyone else seemed to be able to control their limbs and the expressions on their faces, so why couldn't I? Nothing made sense, which increased the pressure, tightened the grip of the vice.

Sometimes I would just scream; a giant blood-freezing sound that would erupt from me like an involuntary sneeze. I would be as surprised to hear it arrive as everyone else around me.

'What the hell did you do that for?' Mum protested the first time she heard the full force of it down the phone extension and practically had a heart attack. 'You nearly broke my eardrum.'

'Sorry, Mum,' I said. 'Couldn't help it.'

I tried to stay cheerful about it, hoping maybe it was all just a phase and would pass as mysteriously as it had arrived, but it frightened me. I was living in a scary world and the last thing I wanted to do was draw attention to myself. But something inside me seemed determined to constantly remind everyone that I was there, that I was different, that I deserved to be given a good kicking. Why couldn't it just shut up and let me fade into the background? Why was it happening? Why me?

The twitches were becoming more violent every day. On top of that I developed some sort of wart-like spots on my neck and chest. The other boys noticed and drew the whole school's attention to them. The camel was now warty – how gross was that? All the other guys were so hard and so cool; they didn't have any room in their lives for a warty, screaming, twitching, camel-faced softy like me.

Just like before I was eventually left with only one friend, but then even he started to imitate and mock me like all the rest of them, behind my back to start with, when he thought I wasn't watching, but eventually to my face. Maybe I was annoying him too and his tolerance had finally run out, or maybe I was embarrassing him and he just didn't want to be seen to like me. There was no escape with the girls here as there had been in previous schools. Their attitude towards what was cool and what was not was much the same as the boys', and I was definitely a 'not'. I didn't fit the culture. I was turning into more and more of a freak every day and the more the pressure built the more my body would react irrationally in response. No one liked me. Being on my own was the safest place to be. Even Mum was getting annoyed.

'For goodness' sake stop that,' she would say in exasperation as I blinked, grimaced and screwed up my face for no apparent reason.

I would try to stop, try to control it, with all my might, and sometimes I could do it for a few minutes, like holding in a cough that is determined to escape, but eventually it would hurt too much and I would have to let it out, like a gigantic clearing of my throat, like the scratching of a really bad itch, like taking an urgent dump or a longed-for wank. Ah, the relief once the obstruction has been blasted away with a mad bark or an ear-splitting scream, until the next time, and the next, and the next.

The flailing of my limbs and torso became more and more exaggerated every day. They had turned from mild tics to violent great twistings of the body. I started the habit of punching myself in the chest and throat, powerful, painful punches that I just couldn't stop myself from doing, leaving my body covered in self-inflicted bruises. I was terrified of being beaten up at school or outside the flat by the other boys, and now I was beating myself up. I wasn't even safe behind my own front door because wherever I went the madman living inside me came too.

Sometimes my lungs would seem to stop working for minutes at a time and I would believe I was going to suffocate. Panic would overwhelm me as I tried to jump start my system again before it stifled me to death. At other times I would hit my windpipe with such force it would make a sound like someone kicking an empty cardboard box down the street.

No matter how much the self-inflicted blows hurt, however, it was better than the pain of trying to hold them in. It could feel like I was going to suffocate if I didn't clear the tension out, but at the same time I was frightened I might break a bone or really damage myself as I tried to punch the obstructions away.

If the tics and twitches were getting on Mum's nerves, you can imagine the effect they were having on the other kids. Boys are meant to conform at that age; anyone who shows they are different had better be tough in order to protect themselves. I wasn't tough. I was just a weedy little kid who could do funny voices, draw funny pictures and do fantastic chicken impersonations.

Did they want to see my Freddy Mercury impression? They did not.

WITH MUM, MY STEPDAD DAVE AND MY BABY BROTHER ALEX.

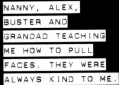

NANNY, ALEX, BUSTER AND GRANDAD TEACHING ME HOW TO PULL FACES. THEY WERE ALWAYS KIND TO ME.

SARAH FELEPPA, HER SISTER EMMA, ME AND LITTLE BRO.
I'M DRESSED AS DARTH VADER (WITHOUT THE MASK).

IN OUR BRIGHTON
BEDSIT. MUM WAS
AT UNI THERE 10
YEARS BEFORE ME!

MAKING UP SONGS
WITH SARAH.
NEITHER OF US
COULD PLAY BUT
WE MANAGED TO
WRITE SONGS
TOGETHER FOR
TURD RADIO.

ABOVE: HAPPY FAMILY AT MUM'S
WEDDING. MY PARTING WAS SO STRAIGHT
MY NICKNAME WAS 'PETER PARTING'.
RIGHT: AT THE RECEPTION PERFORMING
AS FREDDIE MERCURY.

ON A SCHOOL TRIP, AGED 8. MY GOD! IS THAT A BOOK?! MUST BE THE ONLY ONE I'VE EVER READ!

ABOVE: ME (AGED 10) AND MUM (AGED 32).

LEFT: MY SCHOOL PHOTO, AGED 9.

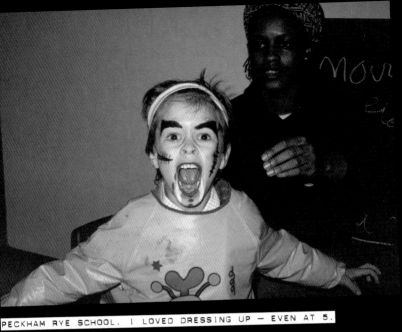

PECKHAM RYE SCHOOL. I LOVED DRESSING UP — EVEN AT 5.

IN FRONT OF THE
BERLIN WALL JUST
BEFORE IT CAME
DOWN. MUM KNEW
IT WAS COMING
DOWN — SHE SAW
IT IN A VISION.

ON PECKHAM COUNCIL ESTATE.
THE BALCONY WAS OUR
PLAYGROUND.

I HAD THREE BABY FRONT TEETH — THE
MIDDLE ONE CAME OUT WHILST MUM AND
I WERE ON HOLIDAY AT CENTRE PARCS,
SHERWOOD FOREST.

DAY TRIP TO WEYMOUTH, AGED 3.
VIRGINIA ASTLEY SAVED MY LIFE
THAT DAY.

WITH MUM AT THE FAIR, AGED 5.
I LOVED SPIDERMAN.

LEFT: MY DAD WHEN MY MUM MET HIM. SHE PINCHED HIS BUM AND SAID 'HELLO, GORGEOUS.'

LEFT: AT TRIDENT STUDIO WHILE MY MUM WAS RECORDING.

ABOVE: WITH MUM ON A TRAIN. TAKEN BY JOHNNY OF THE 'BAND OF HOLY JOY'.

RIGHT: WITH MUM AT THE BRITISH MUSEUM, AGED 18 MONTHS. MUM LIKED EGYPTOLOGY.

Y 9TH BIRTHDAY AT MCDONALD'S WITH TWINS CHARLIE AND ROBIN.

ABOVE: HOSPITAL FOR CHRISTMAS.
YIPPEE! NOT.

LEFT: COOKERY CLASS AT BRISET CENTRE.
DOPED UP TO MY EYES WITH ANTI-TIC
DRUGS BUT GLAD TO BE OUT OF HOSPITAL
AND MAKING A CUP OF CHINA TEA.

PLAYING THE
DRUMS IN THE
STEEL BAND AT
PARKWOOD HALL.

I PAINTED THIS
FOR JIMMY
SOMERVILLE FOR
HIS 40TH WHEN I
WAS 17.

AGED 18, AT HOME WITH MUM
(IN THE MIRROR).

AGED 19, HAVING A GIGGLE WITH
LITTLE BRO ALEX AT DAVE'S
HOUSE (PROBABLY DOING BEAVIS
AND BUTTHEAD IMPERSONATIONS).

Would they find my genie from *Aladdin* act hysterically funny?

Undoubtedly not.

Would they be as amused as baby Alex had been by a musical featuring felt finger puppets?

What do you think?

There was nothing I could do to charm them. They had no reason to be tolerant of my weirdness. I was just a twitching freak who couldn't control himself, virtually begging for a beating.

The whole population of the playground would stand around, pointing and laughing, watching in contempt as I writhed and screamed. They would do impressions of me, competing with one another to be the funniest and the most grotesque.

'Camel, camel, camel!'

I could see what I looked like mirrored in their ugly, hate-filled imitations and I could hear my own horrible noises echoed back at me. There was no possibility of escaping from their attention because the tics and twitches would keep on calling them back, egging them on to new heights of mockery and contempt.

I dreaded every moment of school. I would deliberately miss the bus each morning and go in later so that I would be able to avoid the early morning socializing as everyone jostled for power and position in the social pecking order. My best hope of survival was to stay on the outside, in the shadows, out of sight and earshot as much as possible, but my body wouldn't cooperate, continually struggling to attract people's attention. The harder I fought to control it the more violently it struggled to betray me whenever everyone's attention was distracted by something else, bringing all their eyes swivelling back to me.

Bullies are like junkies, they have to keep increasing the doses to satisfy their urges, to keep their followers amused. What might start as teasing turns to mockery, that grows into casual pushing and pinching, and eventually they want to really hurt you. They want to punish you for being different, teach you a lesson for your audacity in not being like them, and at the same time show everyone else that they are not going to stand for it, that they are going to torture you until you conform and fall under their power. But if you are physically incapable of conforming, if you simply are not able to obey their commands, then they have to increase the pressure, increase the punishment, to teach you a lesson in case anyone else should be bold enough to follow your lead.

There was one boy in particular who wanted to show that he could do anything he wanted to me just because I was a freak. One day he got me in a headlock as I thrashed around helplessly, trying to fight free of him. Everyone was cheering him on as he showed them my blinking, frowning, grimacing face in the crook of his arm, like a trophy he'd brought back from safari, and then he started to insert a pencil up my nostril, like a magician performing a magic trick. He did it just because he could.

He forced it as high as it would go and I was frightened it would break through something and puncture my brain. Was that possible? I had no idea, but I was sure any one of my sudden, jerky movements could have forced it past the point of no return, doing irrevocable damage.

Eventually he decided he had proved his power and he pulled it out, but the rubber, which had been fixed to the end of the pencil, was no longer there. I could feel it, wedged somewhere up behind my eyes, out of reach, a small, dangerous, alien object inside my head. My body went into convulsions, doing everything it could to evict the trespasser, but to no avail. It was stuck.

When I got home and told Mum she rushed me straight up to the hospital. As we waited to be seen by the doctor the staff all seemed to ignore the fact that I was twitching and twisting and punching myself all over the waiting room. Maybe they were just being polite and weren't sure how to react, or maybe they see so many weird sights in a hospital that it didn't strike them as anything special. I could see Mum was really worried and didn't know whether to try to soothe me or get cross with me to try to shock me into pulling myself together. There was nothing she could have done. I was running out of control.

When we finally got to see the doctor he had a good peer around inside my nose, throat and ears and couldn't find the missing rubber.

'I think you must have swallowed it,' he said eventually. 'So it should just work its way through your system now.'

As he sat back from his notes and looked at me appraisingly my body went into one of its biggest ever spasms of activity, throwing me around the room like I was possessed.

'So,' the doctor said to Mum as if none of it was happening, 'apart from the bullying and the rubber incident, is Peter generally in good health?'

'Look at him!' Mum yelled, all her self-control finally deserting her as well. 'What do you think? What the fuck is going on?'

'Shit!' The word exploded out of my mouth. I hadn't seen it coming. I hadn't told it to come. It was like someone else had taken over my voice now as well. What would I lose control of next? The twisting and contorting had never been so bad. It just kept going on and on and I didn't know how I was ever going to stop it. I could see the looks of horror on Mum and the doctor's faces and I tried to regain control, to save at least a tiny bit of my dignity, but it was already a lost battle. There was nothing I could do until my body finally decided to set me free again. I eventually jerked myself to a standstill and sank back into my seat.

Now that Mum had put the whole thing into words, the doctor stopped acting as if he hadn't noticed anything unusual about my behaviour. I found out later that normally they would do all sorts of tests before they would give out any sort of diagnosis in a situation like that, but the doctor was too shocked to be able to follow any normal procedure. When I had finally calmed down enough for him to be able to answer Mum's question he spoke quietly and matter of factly.

'I'm sorry to say, your son has Gilles de la Tourette syndrome.'

'How long will that last?' Mum asked.

'For the rest of his life.'

Mum still cries today when she thinks about that moment, but I was relieved to know that now I had something recognizably wrong with me, the doctors would look after me. They would help me. I wouldn't have to keep fighting the impulses on my own. Someone actually understood what was going on, could actually put a name to it. If they could name it, surely they would be able to cure it.

'What the hell is it?' Mum asked when she had recovered her voice.

'It's more often known just as Tourette's syndrome,' he explained. 'It was first discovered about a hundred years ago by a French doctor called Gilles de la Tourette. It's a neurological disorder which is causing him to have these movements.'

'You mean he can't help it?' Mum asked.

'No.'

Thank God. Now I knew it wasn't something I was just failing to control. It wasn't my fault. It was a 'syndrome'.

As I found out more about Tourette's I realized it explained so much about who I was and what I was able to do. It wasn't just the tics and twitches, but it explained how I was able to do the hallucinogenic voices of the genie in *Aladdin*. It explained why I was always tapping out a beat on any surface my fingers could find. It explained why I was able to do such cool chicken impressions. It explained everything else that started to go wrong and right from that moment onwards.

Just because we now knew what it was, of course, didn't mean we knew what to do about it. I was going to have this thing for the rest of my life and there were going to be other side effects that I hadn't even dreamt about yet, but at least we could try a few things. There were medications I could take, pills that would calm my system down, help me to be more normal. I tried them, keen to go back to being the old Pete, but I didn't like the effects they had on me, feeling frightened I would end up like Jack Nicholson's character at the end of *One Flew Over the Cuckoo's Nest* when they've operated on him and medicated all the personality out of him. I didn't want to be some sort of zombie, travelling through life at half speed – where's the fun in that? Imagine Jim Carrey or Robin Williams slowed down and made normal, what would be the point of that? But I still wanted to be more comfortable. I wanted to be able to control the beast inside me. I wanted to go back to living a normal life.

CHAPTER TEN

THE PADDED CELL

They took me off to a ward in the hospital for observation, to try to work out just how bad things were although they didn't seem to be sure what they were looking for. I was going to be spending a lot of time in hospitals over the next year or two. I would even end up having to spend an entire Christmas there one year, and a hospital Christmas is about as depressing as things can get. Now that Mum had been given an explanation for why I was behaving the way I was she started to remember things from my past, building the picture of how the Tourette's might always have been inside me, waiting for the right moment to increase its hold on my life.

'When you were about two you had some sort of attack in bed one evening,' she remembered. 'You kept twisting and contorting, saying, "It's hurting, Mum! It's tingling." I called an ambulance and they took you up to the hospital but they never found out what it was. So many times you told me you had this tingling sensation in your chest and I would take you to the doctor, thinking maybe you had a chest infection, but they were never able to find anything.'

I knew all about that tingling. Over the years it had grown and grown until now it felt like I was being squeezed to death by a polar bear. The tingling in my own chest would then become transposed in my brain and other people's chests became a problem to me for a while as well. I would find my Tourette's making me fixate on a dirty mark or a button on someone's shirt or blouse, usually the second or third one down. Just looking at it would send me off on an explosion of noises and contortions as I fought with the frustration it had sparked off inside me. There was an acid heartburn advert on the telly at the time which showed this little glowing red thing in just the wrong place on the model's chest and it would send me into a tourettey screaming fit every time I saw it. It felt like they were doing it on purpose just to set my Tourette's off, as if the whole world was conspiring against me, jerking me about like a puppet again for their own sadistic amusement.

One of Mum's friends had a bit of a buxom chest and one day there was a bump in the middle of her bra, which caught my eye and sent the Tourette's spinning out of control. It launched me into a mega-tic, twisting and turning until I eventually ended up bending over with my nose stuck right in her crutch, my whole body frozen, unable to move in any direction, unable to do anything except wait.

Everyone else in the room froze too and just stared at me, waiting for the spasm to release me and allow me to move away.

'Sorry, Lesley,' I said when I was eventually freed and could straighten up. 'I thought I heard something.'

There were laughs to be had from the whole thing, but they never disguised the fact that what was happening to me was a nightmare for all of us.

All sorts of things that had never been a problem before, suddenly became one. Mum got me an accordion to play, for instance, which I really liked, but it covered the part of my chest that I needed to punch, so I had to abandon that, unable to bear the frustration of not being able to clear the constant blockages I believed I could feel. The illness was starting to put limits on the things I was able to do with my life.

When the symptoms became too overpowering, and I would have fits that lasted half an hour or more at a time, Mum would end up calling for an ambulance and they would cart me back up to the hospital to try to calm me down. But even inside the confines of the hospital wards I was a problem to the doctors and nurses. I was not your usual subdued, docile patient who just wants to be nursed quietly and gently back to health. Rather than sitting meekly in bed allowing them to do whatever they wanted, my body would be throwing itself around like a lunatic and they would have to take the metal beds out of the ward because I kept bashing into them and hurting myself. They would put a mattress on the floor for me to lie on and duvets over the sharp corners of the radiators. They were turning the room into a padded cell. Yeah, a padded cell, like I was a complete nutter and a danger to myself. How long before they broke out the straitjackets? Would I end up having to be bound and gagged like Hannibal Lecter?

I guess before Gilles de la Tourette made his discovery there must have been a lot of people in the past who got thrown into padded cells without too many questions being asked, when actually they were suffering from the same sort of thing as me. Imagine what it must have felt like to be locked up as a madman when there was nothing wrong with your mind.

Sometimes the doctors would put me on to a general children's ward, but the other parents didn't like me being there and would complain. They thought it was upsetting for their kids to have to watch me thrashing around and to hear my shouting. They said it was 'disgusting' that I was put in among 'normal' sick kids. Tourette's had given me a strange sort of fixed smile, more of a grimace really, scary, like a death mask or something from a horror film, so perhaps I was a bit of a frightening apparition, until you took the time to get to know me of course,

when you would discover I was the same harmless softy
I had always been.

Mum spent all her time being angry on my behalf
and fighting for my cause. I didn't have the strength to
fight because I was either doped up on Valium-type
drugs or struggling to cope with the symptoms of the
Tourette's itself. I didn't have time to argue with anyone
or to make any unreasonable demands of anyone. I'm
no good at arguing or fighting anyway, I just want to do
fun stuff and have a laugh; I always have and always
will. A bit like my dad and Dave, I suppose. So poor old
Mum was left to fight all my battles for me, and clear up
the mess I made afterwards.

There was one woman who had twin daughters in
the hospital during one of my stays there. They were
about eleven years old and had a thing called Rett
Syndrome, which was much worse than anything I'd ever
seen. It's a brain disorder which only affects girls and
leaves them writhing and helpless all the time, unable to
do anything for themselves, having to be fed through
tubes. They had been normal babies, their mum told us,
but had suddenly changed. At least I hadn't got that. My
brain might have been under attack on a regular basis,
but it hadn't been taken prisoner permanently. The girls
didn't seem to take in anything that was going on
around them at all; they just sat there with their heads
and eyes rolling, so the staff put them in with me. They
had no respite from their disease, ever. Their mother was

nice; she didn't mind how wild I got. I guess she was envious of Mum for having a child who was only weird part of the time. At least Mum and I could talk and do stuff together in my calm moments. She couldn't do anything with her girls except care for them.

I didn't like taking the drugs and there was one male nurse who was always hovering in the background with a syringe when I was having wild spasms, wanting to stick it in my backside, but I never wanted him to. He was like some sinister baddy from the movies lurking in the shadows with his lips pursed and his syringe cocked and primed for action.

'He's not sticking that thing in my arse,' I told Mum, and would muster all my strength to hold the spasm inside. It was like trying to put a lid on a volcano, but I did it, straining every muscle in my body, almost passing out with the effort until the nurse got tired of waiting for his opportunity and flounced off, leaving me free to let a torrent of Tourette's loose again, before eventually dropping on to the mattress in a state of exhaustion.

The doctors told us my Tourette's was the worst case they had ever seen at the hospital, but I don't think they had seen that many of us. One of the nurses refused to come into the room, as she believed I was possessed by the Devil (it was surprising how often the Devil's name cropped up when people saw me in full twitch). The illness really was roaring out of control now, doing my head in as it rampaged through my life, destroying everything in its wake. Sometimes my chest would be jumping up and down as if my heart was trying to make a break for it, like one of those cartoons where a character falls in love and his heart beats so hard it makes his chest thump up and down until it eventually comes bursting out like everything is made of elastic. Sometimes I was frightened the strain would be too much for it: that it would blow a gasket and that would be the end of everything.

Now people were beginning to try to explain to us what had happened in medical history terms, although they didn't seem too sure themselves of the exact facts. The Tourette's, the doctors thought, would probably have come at some point in some form, but all the stress of losing Dave, and the bullying at school and around the estate, had fed the flames, turning up the volume inside my head and pushing me over the edge far more violently and uncontrollably than might otherwise have happened. Had we been living a quiet, orderly, middle-class life, in other words, things might not have got quite so dramatic. It was quite normal, apparently, for the illness not to really make itself known until the patient reached puberty, when the changes going on the body seemed to feed the problem.

I didn't stay on the medication for long because it just made me depressed and sent me to sleep a lot. Sleep was a sort of refuge, but it wasn't an answer to the problem. Eventually I flushed all the pills down the toilet. I wanted to be Pete, whatever that involved, and I wanted to live my own life, however difficult that might be. I didn't want to be sedated, to have my personality taken away just to make me less socially alarming and to be more 'comfortable'. I didn't want to be plodding through life like a zombie, like poor old Richard nailing open the doors in Alice's house. It wasn't a price worth paying. Better to struggle on, because there were still some good moments to be enjoyed in between the bad, some laughs to be had, some drawings to be done.

I discovered that the only time things were calm in my head was when I was concentrating on something creative, like drawing or making music. When I had a pencil in my hand I could pour all my energy into that, channelling it away from the tics and twitches and screams.

Tourette's, however, wasn't the only condition that had blossomed inside me with the arrival of puberty. Other things were changing inside my head at the same time. Before the explosion I had been able to read books and write essays at school, just like any normal, bright kid. I'm not saying I was an avid bookworm or anything, but I used to get As and Bs for my homework. Suddenly I couldn't concentrate on more than a few lines of text at a time and when I tried to write anything I lost the thread of what I was trying to say and the words would jumble up on the page, some of them turning backwards, other ones repeating. It was like I had acquired dyslexia where I'd never had it before. The doctors said that wasn't possible when Mum suggested it to them, that you were either born with it or not, but they didn't have any other explanation for the changes.

The experts also told me I had Attention Deficit Disorder (ADD), which was why I was finding it hard to concentrate on things. Maybe that had already been evident with the petit mals Lizzie-Anne and Kaye had noticed all those years before, but now it was taking on other forms, like it was mutating. I was finding it hard to talk like I had before, hard to make conversation in the same constant, flowing way. Once upon a time I could sit chatting at Mum, or anyone else who would listen, for hours, just babbling on like any normal child. Now I didn't seem to be able to find the right words in time, or they would trip over one another in their anxiety to get out of my head, so I would fall silent and drift off into a world of my own. I had always liked daydreaming and staring into space, but in the past I had always been able to bring myself back to Earth if someone tried to talk to me; not any more. Mum would be trying to get through and I would only be able to answer in monosyllables.

Maybe a lot of boys at that age have something similar happen, talking in grunts, sighs and tuts whenever they're addressed by adults – like Harry Enfield's 'Kevin' character – but that is normally a matter of choice, saved for parents and teachers. This was something happening way beyond my control. Within the space of a couple of months it seemed like I had become a different person. But I hadn't, it was still me inside. I was still the same Pete.

It was normal, the doctors told us, for puberty to bring on the major symptoms with Tourette's – as if a guy doesn't have enough to worry about when every single thing about his body seems to be changing every few hours anyway. My puberty had arrived like a steam train, smashing through my head, my body and my life, destroying everything in its wake.

They told Mum I was worse when she was around, and maybe I was because I was trying harder to communicate and to suppress everything when she was there than when I was on my own, but it was an unkind thing to tell her. What was she supposed to do – desert me? I wanted my mum to be there, I didn't want them to tell her to stay away, just because my tics subsided when she wasn't there. On that basis I would have to have sat alone in my padded cell for the rest of my life, avoiding any stimulation and company that might excite the monster inside me and cause him to act up. That wasn't the sort of life I wanted. I wanted to be back out there, having some fun, partying.

It was doubly hard for Mum because as soon as I came out of hospital she would have to deal with me on her own, with no professional back-up at all and no partner to share the strain and the worry, to take me off her hands from time to time to give her a break. Whenever she asked for help or guidance the doctors would tell her I was her responsibility. She was more than willing to take on that responsibility, she just wanted a bit of advice and back-up. She also had Alex to look after and he was a bit of a handful by then. He was not the same sort of placid, smiley kid I had been – although he is now – he was a right little screamer, so she had him going on at her in one ear and me shouting and yelling in the other, and having fits that could last anything up to fifteen minutes as I rolled around on the floor, bucking and punching. There must have been times when she must have thought she was the one going mad.

I had developed another alarming habit when I was at home where I would launch myself at her or Alex or the cat as they went about their normal business, letting out a great wail, and pinning them to the floor. I would know I was about to do it and I would be apologizing all the time we were stuck there, but I still couldn't stop myself. They all reacted pretty much the same. They would go a bit wide-eyed with fear and then they too would freeze and wait until my frozen muscles relaxed and were willing to let them go. We would then all just get on with whatever we had been doing before the Tourette's had made me pounce. I was lucky the cat never decided to take my eyes out during one of these attacks – maybe he realized I couldn't help it as well.

One day Mum was talking on the phone, trying to sort out my schooling, when I was seized by a gigantic contortion as I walked past. My hand swung towards my chest but accidentally caught Mum on the back of her neck, knocking her out cold for a few seconds. Her life must have been pretty shit most of the time during those years, a bit like living in her own padded cell, and it wasn't going to get any better for a while as more and more new symptoms kept pouring out of my mental closets.

BOLLOCKS!

Looking after me was more than a full-time job, particularly with Alex there as well, and Mum had virtually no moment to herself to earn any money during those years. We were constantly broke and struggling to pay the next bill. Some people would say it was all her fault for choosing to be a 'single mother', but neither Dad nor Dave had ever worked when they were with her, and I doubt if either of them would have wanted to put up with me screaming and spasming all over the place anyway. So we wouldn't have been any better off, even if she'd stuck to one or other of them like glue. And she wasn't left with much time to meet anyone new either; it's hard to start a romantic relationship when you have a full-grown son throwing himself around the house, pinning you to the ground every so often or knocking you out when you're making a phone call.

Getting me to and from different doctors and appointments was another drain on our non-existent resources, but Mum always agreed to see anyone who might help me, willing to follow up any lead she could find. Public transport was a bit of a nightmare for me, and for everyone else in the vicinity, so she often had to spend her money on taxis just to get me to appointments in a reasonably relaxed state. But however hard it was, she never wavered in her support, even though many of the trips turned out to be worse than useless once we got there.

She managed to get me in to see the country's leading expert on Tourette's, Dr Mary Robertson at the National Hospital of Neurology. Dr Robertson had written several books on the subject, and has just produced a new one (*Why Do You Do That?* co-written with Dr Uttom Chowdhury), which is aimed at explaining to other children why Tourette's sufferers are like they are. There were a few kids I knew who I would have liked to have given it to – fat chance they would ever have read it though! The kind of guys who gave me a hard time in the playground were not the type who were likely to read a book just for the pleasure of increasing their understanding of why 'monkey-face' was such a freak. More likely they would have rolled it up and inserted it in my nostril.

When we got to the hospital I realized immediately that the waiting room was filled with fellow sufferers all queuing for their appointments. One of the symptoms of the illness is that we all tend to copy what the others do, so when one guy started doing his shoelace up the rest of us followed, and when I shouted 'Bollocks!' it turned into a sort of foul-mouthed choral event. I think they call it 'echolalia' (echo tongue). It's great needing a whole Latin dictionary just to describe all the stuff that's wrong with you.

Dr Robertson was as brilliant as her reputation promised. She understood everything we told her, nodding and taking notes all the time, and everything she said back to us about the condition we recognized. I immediately liked her and felt she understood completely what was going wrong in my head. She had seen it all a hundred times before in one form or another. There were always other experts from around the world sitting in on the consultations when I went to see her, listening in and learning from this great world authority. Mum had sort of bluffed her way in to see her and had somehow managed to jump the usual year-long waiting list, but once we had met her, Dr Robertson told us she intended to stay on my case.

She said it was one of the most severe examples of Tourette's she had ever come across and asked permission to film me as I stood in the middle of the room howling uncontrollably like a wolf. Shit, man! I was making a bit of medical history now. She told Mum that a lot of sufferers became very bitter and nasty as a result of having the symptoms ruining their lives, and she thought it was cool that I still seemed to be friendly towards everyone and to have a zest for life. Tourette's had given me a way of hugging people, incorporating a bit of a tic, which left them knowing that they'd been hugged, but it was very affectionate and mostly they seemed to like the experience. Well, Dr Robertson did anyway. She said she wanted me to trying going back on some of the medication again, and because I trusted her I agreed.

Not everyone we saw, however, was as brilliant as her. There was one psychologist (I think he called his system 'Gestalt'), who believed that he should stay silent throughout the consultation and I would then be able to tell him all about myself and my feelings.

'This is a time for Peter to speak when he wishes to,' he announced ponderously in Mum's direction.

So he sat in silence, staring at me, rubbing his chin thoughtfully as I twisted and turned, screaming and shouting and punching myself. He gave no reaction, no feedback, asked no questions, as if he was trying to show me that nothing I could do would shock or surprise him; like that was my big goal in life. He was really scary. At the next session he observed Mum and Alex as well, seeing how we interacted as a family group. At the end of that session he told us that he had decided there were too many men in Mum's life, even though they were mostly gay and all just our friends, and that that was what was causing me confusion. He was also convinced there were 'too many teeth' on the monster that Alex had been busily drawing as he waited for the silence and the embarrassment to end.

'That's not a monster,' Alex told him indignantly. 'That's Zippy from *Rainbow*. That's his zip, not teeth.'

Ignoring Alex's contemptuous stare, the learned doctor continued on his path to the conclusion that every one of my tics was caused by a fantasy, 'either violent or sexual'.

'Are they?' Mum asked me as soon as we were out of the room, looking both surprised and intrigued.

'Of course they're not!' I replied. Like I ever had time to fit in a fantasy before spinning round a room like a top.

When Mum told Dr Robertson what the psychologist had suggested she got really worried, saying that such theories had been discredited years before. All the experts in the room agreed with her, shaking their heads in a worried fashion, and jotting down more notes. So I didn't have to go and see the creepy Gestalt man any more after those two sessions, which saved us a few taxi fares and a lot of wasted time and effort.

Having been force-fed so much information about this whole new world of Tourette's, Mum threw herself into doing as much as she could for the Tourette's Syndrome Association. Since her main expertise was in street theatre and music, she persuaded a friend who was the costumier from *Les Miserables* to create her a Christmas tree costume, complete with twinkling fairy lights and dangling balls on its branches. She wrote a song and made a CD and went back out on to the streets, busking in venues like Trafalgar Square, collecting money for the cause and selling copies of the CD. Being a human Christmas tree got her lots of publicity, and she even got her picture in *The Times*; my mum the campaigner!

The 'Shit!' I had shouted at the doctor on the day we discovered what was wrong with me was the first sign of yet another problem occurring. The technical name for it is 'coprolalia', which basically means 'crappy tongue' in posh Latin doctor-speak. Or just plain old 'potty-mouth' maybe. Not all Tourette's sufferers do it, but I seemed to be doing virtually everything available on the menu, the complete package, although I never started spitting, which some people do – but it's never too late to develop something new, so maybe that's something we can all look forward to.

Anyway, behind that first 'shit' there was a whole library of swear words just queuing up for their turn to be the next unwelcome arrival. Whatever you want to call the problem the result is the same: whatever word I shouldn't be using is the one word my whole brain and body longs to spit out. I could no more resist the impulse to shout them out at the top of my voice than I could fight the urge to tic and squirm, clear my throat, blink, grimace or punch myself. All the anger and frustration that had built up in my system as a result of the illness had to escape. There had to be a way of sending it out into the world, and swear words were the missiles needed to shoot the venom out of the mother-ship, to sweep the imaginary blockage from the system and relieve the ache, if only for a few seconds. It is a bit like when you have a cold and you have to blow your nose, sneeze, cough or clear your throat; there is no choice and the action relieves the irritation or pain for a moment, but a few seconds later you have to do the same thing again, over and over again, as your body's defence mechanism tries to empty itself of the virus or infection.

Whatever natural barriers most of us have to stop totally unsuitable words popping out at even more unsuitable moments just don't work in my brain. The wrong chemicals maybe, the wrong electrical impulses, whatever the technical reason the words that small boys are normally taught to keep corralled in a safe place, only to be let out when they are with other small boys, just refused to stay cooped up in my head. Every time I would think I had managed to round one escapee up, another would make a break for freedom. As if the visual effect of all my expressions and gestures wasn't enough to frighten innocent passers-by, I now accompanied them with a soundtrack that could stop an entire shop full of people in their tracks, cut through the dialogue of any movie in any cinema, turn heads down the whole length of a bus and both startle and embarrass everyone within earshot.

'Bollocks!' was the favourite for a long time, exploding out at every possible opportunity, accompanied by a swift punch to the windpipe.

I would try to fight it if I thought I was somewhere where I would cause too much offence, but
not usually with much luck. Walking down the street
with Mum one day I was aware that there was an
elderly lady walking behind us with a stick and that she
was about to overtake as I struggled to hold in the word.
But she wasn't walking fast enough and I couldn't get
my body to move away to a respectable distance. The
stress was building inside my head as she drew closer
and closer, and I thought I was going to explode as
she shuffled past with an endless slowness. It was no
good. I was losing my grip on it. I couldn't hold it a
second longer.

'BOLLOCKS!' I erupted, punching myself hard, every
ounce of my suppressed energy pouring out through this
break in the dam.

'I'm so sorry,' Mum said to the startled-looking
woman.

'That's quite all right my dear,' she replied. 'I've
been longing to shout that myself for years.'

Every so often I would meet people like that and I
would realize that the world could be a kinder and more
understanding place than I had so far experienced. If I
could just find a corner where the good people with open
minds ruled, where they thought unusual people were
funny, interesting and life enhancing rather than threatening or disgusting, where I wouldn't be marked out as
someone who needed to be ostracized and punished,

then all would be well. South London, however, was never going to be that paradise.

At one time I developed a habit of howling like a wolf and barking like a dog. The monkey and the camel had now gone canine on me. Just like the swearing I could only hold the howls in for a short time before they had to escape. Going to any public place like a cinema or theatre was always a problem, because I didn't want to disturb the other people sitting close by, but I refused to allow it to make me a complete outcast. Every so often, when there was a movie I really wanted to see, I would muster all my courage and go. I went with Mum and Alex to watch *The Empire Strikes Back*, the whole family having become fans of *Star Wars* by then. We were sitting in the front row and the Wookie kept letting off howls. I worked out that if I waited until he was about to let rip I could get my own howl out at the same time, causing minimum annoyance to other people. It also relieved my echolalia, the urge to join in. It became a bit of a joke with the rest of the audience in the cinema by the end, especially in the final scene, where they all get awarded their medals, when I was able to stand up and really let it all out along with Chewbacca.

'That was so great that people were laughing and clapping you,' Mum said as we came out. 'I was terrified we were going to get a load of abuse as usual. I thought they would complain you were ruining the film but they loved you. They actually saw the funny side instead of getting cross.'

As well as having coprolalia (shit tongue), I also have copropraxia (shit movements), and there were times when I couldn't see a peephole in a door without giving it the finger, just couldn't resist the urge. I can't explain it, but neither can the doctors or the psychologists or any of the other experts who have gazed into the world of Tourette's and come away scratching their heads. It is a mystery to us all.

It was a constant battle for Mum, trying to get officials and experts to listen to her, to understand what was going on and why she needed help in managing me. She wanted to get me a 'statement of special needs' so I could go to a school that understood how to help me, but the authorities didn't want to help. They said I 'only' had Tourette's and I should be able to cope in a normal school.

'How can he cope?' Mum would yell at them. 'Look at him! His body's chucking itself all round the place, he can't even sit at a desk for more than a few minutes. He's shouting out swear words every few seconds. How can he attend a normal school? How is that fair on him or the other kids in the class who are trying to learn?'

It was important to get me statemented before I was sixteen, because after that I would be past the school leaving age and the state wouldn't take any more

responsibility for helping me. If I could get statemented, however, they were legally obliged to help me out
with education and training until I was nineteen. We
needed all the support and assistance we could get.
Other kids may be ready to go out into the world when
they leave school at seventeen or eighteen, but I needed to buy as much extra time as possible in order to try
to work out how to manage my illness and all its
colourful symptoms.

Now that I was ill I really wanted my dad to know what
had happened to me. It didn't seem right that he didn't
even know what I had been going through, and that
Mum had to do everything for me without his support.
Half my DNA had come from him, so maybe he would
be able to understand me better than most other people.
I really wanted to see him again. My memory of the last
time we met was no longer very sharp and I wanted to
remind myself what he was like, to understand a bit
more about where I had come from. I told Mum what I
wanted to do and she was very good about it. She had
lost touch with him completely over the years, but she
asked around among some mutual friends and someone
promised to tell him that I wanted to talk to him.
He phoned back within about half an hour, which made
me feel good, like maybe I wasn't as separated from him
as I had thought if I could reach out to him this easily.

He asked how I was in the normal polite manner, but trying to tell him through the torrent of nervous noises and swear words made me burst into tears. How do you explain in a phone call how your whole life has exploded and changed out of all recognition? How do you convey the agony of the condition and the tedium of all the visits to doctors and experts? Where could I start to talk about all the tiny steps forward in understanding that had happened over the previous months to someone who didn't even know I was ill until half an hour before? Pretty much impossible really.

Dad said he thought he could understand a bit of what I was going through, having had a lot of strange things going on in his own head for years – was this part of my problem, was it all about genetics and DNA? He told me he had a job working with patients in a children's mental hospital, so maybe he did have a bit more of an insight into my world than I had first thought.

Something in our conversation must have triggered his interest because he came and took me out a few days later. We went for a walk together around Greenwich. It felt very different being out with my dad than out on my own. I didn't feel remotely threatened by anyone or anything. He still looked really cool and I liked the fact that I could see I looked like him. It feels good to be able to see where you've come from, where you fit in to the whole universal order, where the DNA has travelled from. After wandering around for a while we decided to pop into a pub (I guess if I'd been old enough to get away with going into a pub the last time we met we wouldn't have had to bother with the graveyard), and Dad had a few too many drinks, which didn't impress Mum when we arrived back home with Dad pogoing down the street and kicking a massive beer glass into the air.

He then pretended to miss his last train, a story that didn't convince Mum for a second, and spent the night on the sofa. Deep inside I wondered if maybe this was the start of something new. Maybe now we would be able to stay together and be a proper family. He must have been feeling something as well because he invited me to go on holiday with him to meet his mum, my other gran, who I hadn't seen or heard from since I was ten months old. I didn't know much about her, except that she'd previously been a mayoress but had won the lottery and moved to live near the beach.

Mum used to tell me about the first time she met Dad's parents when she and Dad started seeing each other. She managed to make them sound very intriguing.

'This is my husband,' my gran had said, pointing to my grandad. 'He's going out with a sixteen-year-old at the moment because it's his last chance to feel a pair of firm tits.' Mum was already gobsmacked but the best was yet to come. 'Do feel free to have the run of the house,' Gran told her, grandly. 'Go anywhere you like but I must warn you that every afternoon at four o'clock is my time; that's when I have a private appointment with Wagner and no one must come into the sitting room.'

Apparently she kept a dildo on the coffee table and every afternoon she put 'Ride of the Valkyries' on the stereo. Even Mum, who prided herself on being pretty open-minded and had seen most things, was shocked. The holiday was all a bit weird, but I still had a nice time. They had a cute dog called Boppy, which reminded me how much I'd missed having a dog of my own since Lassie had been driven away.

I felt confident Dad and I would stay in touch after that. We made a date for him to come and see me again, but he didn't turn up. His girlfriend phoned later to say he'd been in a terrible motorway accident and even told Mum which hospital he'd been taken to with a broken back. Apparently the doctors were worried he might never walk again. When I nagged Mum to phone the casualty department of the hospital to find out how he was, they said they'd never heard of him. She phoned his girlfriend back and Dad answered the phone.

'I can't believe it,' Mum said when she realized the whole thing was a lie. 'I thought you were supposed to have broken your back.'

'Go take a big hairy one up the arse,' he slurred, and that was the last time we heard from him until I went into the *Big Brother* house, apart from the odd unintelligible, sentimental phone call in the small hours of the morning, which always resulted in Mum hanging up on him. I could see we couldn't hope for any help from that branch of the cavalry. My spirits were sinking fast.

THOUGHTS OF SUICIDE

Deciding that she had to get back to work at least part time now that Alex was getting bigger and going to school, Mum and a couple of her friends formed a new group called Brilliant Strings. Things were going quite well for them and sometimes she was even earning five or six hundred pounds a day on the odd days when she was working, which made it more practical to be able to pay for childcare. If she did have to be away for more than a day at a time, like when she got a few days' work backing the Manic Street Preachers, she had to find someone who could stay with me, like I was still a little kid who needed babysitting. It was humiliating for a boy who should have been old enough to be taking on some of the childcare for her. I should have been able to look after Alex, but as it was I was now more of a liability than he was.

We had some neighbours in our block called Mary and Andy who were really lovely, and I used to stay with them whenever I could. Andy kept a tank full of lizards in their living room, giant great flesh-eating things some of them, and I loved them. There's something very peaceful and zen about lizards, the way they just stare out at the world, only lashing into action at the last minute when they see something juicy to eat or sense danger and need to run away. They waste no excess energy. It must be great to be that in control of your movements, to be that cool. I would have given anything to be more like them.

I felt so sad about the way my life was falling to pieces. Nothing seemed to be working out. Dave had gone from our lives and Dad had obviously lost interest again. I was still in a really crap school where everyone hated me, and I was living on a horrible council estate, surrounded by frightening people who wanted to beat me up. On top of all that the doctors were telling me the Tourette's, which was making my life so stressful and uncomfortable, would never go. I had the choice of being drugged up and permanently zombified, or ticcing and twitching for all eternity. My life, it seemed, was going to be shit forever.

I had held on to my optimism and high spirits for as long as I possibly could, but now I was beginning to wonder if there was any point in going on. Just two years before my life had been going OK. I'd liked the way I looked and most people in the real world had seemed to warm to me, even if they hadn't at school. I'd been good at school subjects on the whole, enjoying the buzz that I got from art and music. OK, I wasn't one of the most popular guys in the playground but I wasn't being beaten to a pulp all the time either, or having pencils shoved up my nose, and I wasn't some sort of freak show that drew crowds in the street, made normally decent people feel they needed to protect their children from me and made less decent ones want to attack me or lock me up somewhere.

The Tourette's was exhausting me, wearing me down, draining my life spirit away. I could also see just how much of a strain I was putting on Mum. She was having to look after me at the same time as bringing up Alex, worrying about money all the time, trying to work and having no life of her own. I was just a burden to her, not able to help in any way. I started to think that it would be better to simply end things myself now in order to make life easier for all of us. If they were saying I was going to be like this for the rest of my life, I didn't feel I had the energy to put up with it any more. I had loved life so much when I was little, and now it seemed so hateful.

Every few weeks I would have a prolonged attack of spasms that was so bad and so frightening Mum would call an ambulance and I would be taken back in to the hospital, sedated and put under observation again, but they still never really seemed to know what they were looking for. No one was even pretending that they held out any hope of finding a cure. Once they'd calmed me down, after a few days, when I was back to just ticcing and punching myself the usual amount, they would let me back out into the world, reminding Mum once again that I was her responsibility. I don't think she ever forgot that fact for even a second, but they seemed to think they had to keep refreshing her memory, like she was a naughty child trying to shirk doing her homework. I suppose they had her down as an irresponsible single mother who was trying to pass the burden of her sick son off on to the State. Their attitude made her angry a lot of the time, which usually led to her speaking her mind, which tended to make them disapprove of her even more. Mum can be quite outspoken when she's annoyed, and people don't always like that.

We were still living in the top-floor flat in Greenwich and I would sit on the balcony and stare down at the concrete below, imagining what it would feel like to jump. Would it hurt? Would I definitely kill myself and be released from everything, or would I end up crippling myself for life on top of everything else? I'd heard about Christopher Reeve, the actor who had played Superman, who had fallen off his horse a couple of years before and ended up a helpless quadriplegic, unable to move a single muscle, completely dependent on other people for everything; I didn't want to end up like that. People say committing suicide is a coward's way out, but I think it takes a fair bit of courage to throw yourself over a precipice into the unknown like that.

One day Mum had popped across the road to the shops for some milk. It was the first time she had left me on my own without a babysitter; she thought I would be okay for a few minutes. I saw this as an opportunity to solve all our problems if I acted quickly and decisively. I pulled myself up on the edge of the balcony and paused, taking a few seconds to prepare myself for a final flight. At that moment Mum came back into the flat and saw me sitting there, plucking up the final ounce of courage to do it. I don't know if I would ever have had the nerve to actually jump, but if I'd had one of my big tics at that moment I would have been propelled over the side in a second anyway. Sometimes the tics would grab my whole body and throw me back several feet like I'd been zapped by some invisible superhero. If that had happened at that moment the decision whether or not to jump would have been taken out of my hands. But for some strange reason my Tourette's had chosen that moment to fall still, almost as if it knew that something more important was about to happen and it was showing respect. Perhaps the invisible alien monster felt that its work was done; its mission on Earth had been completed and it had finally succeeded in driving me over the edge, just taking a few seconds to sit back and enjoy the show's finale.

'Oh my God, what are you doing?' Mum croaked, hardly daring to breathe in case she triggered a rogue spasm and sent me spinning away into oblivion.

'I want to kill myself, Mum,' I said, and started sobbing because I didn't really want to go through with it, I just didn't want to have to go on the way I was. 'I'm nothing but a fucking freak now. I used to think that one day I would get married and have a family and a career but now my whole life has been ruined.'

When I saw her face and heard her pleading with me to get off the railing I realized I was being selfish and allowing myself to wallow in self-pity. If I jumped I wouldn't actually be lightening the burden on her at all, I would be loading her up with grief and guilt and God knows what else, and I would be depriving Alex of his strangely entertaining big brother. The Tourette's was my problem and I couldn't just get rid of it by ending my life, I had to keep going. I had to find a way of beating it, even if the doctors couldn't help with a cure.

'I can't do it,' I said, climbing back down, 'because I've got you and I know you would never get over it if I did.'

Having been alerted to the possibility that I could throw myself off the balcony, or that my Tourette's could do it for me, even if my nerve failed, Mum started a new crusade to get us moved down to the ground floor of the block. Everything to do with the council was always such a battle, filling out forms, arguing with officials who couldn't give a toss about anyone, trying to convince people that we needed help. The fact that she was a single mum made it all the harder; officials always seem to listen to men more than they do to women. Wankers!

The council sent someone round to see us, to assess whether we really did need to be moved or whether we were just trying it on. While the woman was sitting there I went into a sort of trance, a new version of the petit mals I'd had as a small kid, just staring into space, my thoughts floating away as if I wasn't joined to my physical body, feeling unable to force my mind to come back to Earth and engage with this woman.

'Doesn't look like there's anything wrong with him to me,' she told Mum, obviously believing that we were time-wasting spongers, expecting the State to give us whatever handouts we asked for.

'Pete?' Mum said, her voice pleading with me to come back from wherever it was I'd drifted off to.

'What!? What!?' I barked, landing back in the living room from my dream state with a bang, coughing and punching myself hard to try to clear things through so I could pay attention to whatever it was this woman wanted to say to me.

'You did that on purpose,' the woman accused Mum as she watched me writhing around fighting to get control of myself and trying to concentrate. 'You made him do that.'

She refused to listen to any more, having decided we'd staged the whole thing, and went away to mark us down as the lowest possible priority for moving. Once the decision had been made there was no arguing with them. We were officially listed as time-wasters and so we had to stay at the top of the block. From then on Mum was constantly panicking every time she saw me going near the balcony doors. I tried to convince her that I had realized the error of my ways and wouldn't try it again, but I could understand why she could never completely put her fears to rest now that they had been stirred up with a picture of her child throwing himself to his death.

Every new tic my brain thought up seemed to be designed to make my life more difficult. I had one that would wait until I was just about to take a sip from a cup or a glass before jerking into life and tipping the drink all over me. Or I would be getting stuck into a meal that I was really looking forward to and the next thing I would know it would be dripping all over my head, or I would have speared myself in the neck with the fork, having forgotten to drop it before giving myself a punch. There could sometimes be some laughs to be had from the slapstick of it all – a kind of 'Norman Wisdom meets Freddie Star on speed' scenario, but it was also mega scary.

I made sure I always held my knife in my left hand, knowing that the punches would invariably come from the right and believing it would be better to impale myself on the prongs of a fork than the blade of a knife, although not too great an option either way to be honest.

It was like having some tireless practical joker living in my head, someone who never slept and never saw when their jokes had gone too far and were starting to piss their audience off. If I'm cutting vegetables, or something where I have to use my right hand, I just have to drop the knife the moment I feel a tic coming on.

The same happened when I was holding a pen once as well, an unexpected tic driving it into my neck so deeply I couldn't get it out without help. A number of times I only narrowly missed stabbing myself in the eye with some implement or other.

Nearly all of the stuff my brain would tell me to do was bizarre. Mum walked in one morning as I was getting dressed and found me wagging a scolding finger at one of my socks.

'What are you doing?' she asked, trying to stifle a laugh.

'Dunno,' I admitted. 'I just know I've got to tell my clothes to fuck off before I put them on.'

Sometimes the demented joker would take over control of my whole body and send it off in a direction I didn't want to go in, like a *Road Runner* cartoon. One moment I would be walking down the street beside Mum, knowing exactly where we were both planning to go, then suddenly my legs would swerve round a corner and I would be heading off in a completely different direction.

'Pete, Pete,' I would hear Mum calling after me, 'we're going this way!'

'I know, Mum, I know,' I would wail over my shoulder. 'I'll be right there, just waiting for the wind to change.'

Sometimes there could be a comic side to everything, but at other times Alice was right and it was like being possessed by the Devil. I was staying in a house once, belonging to some people who were a bit fussy about their possessions and obviously worried about the damage I might do to their lovely home. The stress of trying to keep control of every movement and avoid accidents was building and building in my head as they told me not to do that, not to touch this, and eventually my body detonated involuntarily into action and tried to get under the bed in my room, like a panic-stricken dog frantic to escape from a thunderstorm, cramming my head into a gap far too small for it, legs and arms scrabbling desperately to force it further under.

'Help me, Mum, help me!' I shouted.

She tried to pull me back out but there was nothing she could do, the enemy was too strong. I was too strong. She called an ambulance and the attack was still going on by the time they got there. The shocked ambulance men tried to haul me out but the force of the Tourette's sent one of them flying across the room. My chest was leaping like it had just had an electric shock administered. The men eventually managed to get me into the ambulance, pinning me down as I thrashed frantically around. They injected something in to relax my muscles and the demons finally gave up, allowing me to go limp, but Mum told me later my chest was still jumping even after the rest of my body fell still.

If your body is capable of doing that to you, with so much violence that it hurts, it's frightening to imagine what else it might do without stopping to ask for permission or checking the wisdom of its actions. That day it just decided to get under a bed, but what if another day it decided to run out into the road in front of a speeding car? Supposing it decided to take a running jump over a cliff? How would I stop it? We all rely on being able to be in charge of our actions, and to not be in control was pretty much the same thing as being mad. If I was going to be a nutter, I wanted it to be in a way chosen by me, a deliberate eccentricity, not in a way chosen by an alien. I was back at the hospital one day, trying to get a meal from the plate into my mouth while my body was letting rip, doing everything it could to prevent me. I was sobbing with frustration as I tried to calm it down so I could just eat something, when a woman I didn't recognize passed by. I was making a bit of a spectacle of myself, howling like a wolf and all the rest of the Tourettey-Pete Show, and she stopped to watch and ask Mum a bit about me. In the course of the conversation Mum explained how she was trying to get us moved to a ground floor flat and described what our lives were like. The woman started to cry. Mum had no idea who she was but seeing her tears made Mum cry as well. It turned out she was the manager of the local Social Services.

When she heard that we had been accused of making our story up she seemed to literally bristle with indignation. Within a week she had kicked a lot of arse and we found ourselves moving to the ground floor of our block.

It was a relief for Mum. The only problem was that the previous tenant had been a heroin dealer and his regular customers kept turning up at all hours of the day and night, none of them willing to believe that we couldn't sell them what they were craving. When we first moved in there was mess and discarded needles everywhere. There was blood on the walls and shit smeared all over the bathroom. There was even still some of their gear hidden down the back of the cistern, the whole gruesome *Trainspotting* scene.

Andy, our neighbour with the lizards, knew how much I liked animals and had given me a little tabby kitten called Bullseye. I'd re-christened him Tommy. He had a lovely nature and became my best friend in the long days that I spent not going anywhere. So when I had a dream that he was going to die I was horrified, knowing how often my dreams came true. I didn't like having these visions, feeling frightened that one day I would dream Mum was going to die, not being sure how I would cope with knowing that, waiting for the axe to fall, wondering where it would come from. Shit! Something like that could drive you mad for real, couldn't it?

For some reason Mum got an urge to go down the shops and buy some flowers a few days later. As she came back a neighbour shouted out that there was a dead cat in the road and that she thought it was Tommy. Mum came running into the house crying and telling me what had happened. Like a miracle my Tourette's seemed to arrest itself, a strange calmness settling over me as I did what had to be done. I went outside to fetch him. Then I sat for ages, stroking him, before going back outside and digging him a grave. When I'd finished Mum laid the flowers she had just bought on top of it, along with a statue of the cat god and lots of lanterns, creating a shrine like the one we'd visited on the Walsingham pilgrimage. I kept a vigil by the grave for nearly a week, sitting very still, just thinking about life and death, not feeling like talking to anyone, occasionally twitching and swearing quietly to myself, trying to make some sense of the whole life and death thing.

SPECIAL PLACES

If I couldn't go to a normal school, and I was very happy to agree with Mum on that if it meant I never had to set foot in Thomas Tallis again in my life, where could I go?

I was still too young to leave school and I had no qualifications at all, so no one in their right minds would have given me a job anyway, even if I hadn't been touretting like a maniac. The Tourette's had struck before I had even had a chance to do my GCSEs. What chance would I have in the world without a single certificate to my name? What chance did I have of getting anywhere in the world anyway as long as I was yelling out swear words and punching myself all the time? The mainstream, working world has pretty strict rules about behaviour most of the time. It might be possible to get away with the things I did when I was walking around the open streets, where people could escape from me if I alarmed them, but it wouldn't be the same in a confined space. Employers tend not to want to hire people who are blatantly unable to obey the basic rules of etiquette, people who might drive away customers and embarrass fellow workers. Office workers might not have to wear bowler hats and carry umbrellas to work any more, but they are still expected to be vaguely normal. There must be exceptions out there, I told myself, people who would be able to see the old Pete behind the apparent nutter, but how would I find them? And what skills could I offer them, even if I had been old enough and qualified for anything?

I had, in effect, become disabled almost overnight. But would I fit into that category either? There are ramps for wheelchairs all over the place but not many allowances for swearing twitchers. Did I have to be in any category? Why couldn't I just be myself? Why couldn't I be Pete? But I wasn't even sure I knew who Pete was any more, especially since he kept changing his behaviour every week, becoming more and more difficult to live with.

The frustration inside me was growing all the time as I desperately tried to hold all my urges in check, tried to conform, tried not to alarm people. I could never keep it up for long, not without running a serious risk of bursting a blood vessel.

I could see no way out of the trap, no way to move forward. There were so many things I loved doing. I loved my art, I loved my music and I loved to dance. I actually loved life, even though it seemed to be doing its best to end our love affair. There had to be openings for someone with those attributes, surely?

Despite spending months banging on doors and making innumerable phone calls, Mum eventually had to agree to sending me to a place called Briset as a 'temporary measure'. It was called a 'pupil referral unit' – what did that mean? It seemed to mean it was a sanctuary for anyone who was having trouble at school, either because they had a problem like mine, or because they were being bullied for some other reason, or because they just didn't fit into any of the right moulds.

The moment I got there my life took on a new pattern and in many ways it was quite restful, removing a lot of the difficulties of normal life from my shoulders. I had now become 'special' because someone had realized I had 'special needs', even though I still hadn't been officially statemented.

Each day I was picked up from outside the flat in a van full of other people with their own particular special needs, and taken to and from the centre for the day. It felt safe once I was in the van, surrounded by other damaged people, protected from the lurking dangers of the streets around the flat and around my old school. It was nice to be cocooned, but at the same time I hated the idea that I needed to be removed from real life, that I couldn't cope, that even in this small way I had been recognized as not being normal any more. Although I had always been interested in weird and different people, and wanted to be like that myself, I didn't want that to mean I had to be separated off, even if it was for my own protection.

Briset was so different to Thomas Tallis, or any other school I had been to, it might as well have been a different planet; a friendly, benign planet. This was not a jungle, run on the principle of survival of the fittest. This was altogether softer and more caring, more nurturing. No one there expected me to be able to cope on my own in the battle against life's challenges.

It didn't take me long to make friends because I could understand how most of the other people felt since they had been through similar experiences to me. There were also kids there who had inconvenienced and embarrassed the outside world by getting pregnant too early, and schoolphobics who couldn't handle school at all, and kids who had problems because their mums were dying, all sorts. Because we all had problems and worries of our own, most of us were less quick to judge other people, more accepting of each other's differences and difficulties. There were only about twenty-five of us in the whole school and we were all there for a reason, all in the same boat, which made it feel nice and comradely. I didn't feel threatened at all. It was safe, a temporary respite while I tried to work out what the hell to do with my life and waited to see what my illness would transform itself into next.

I made some good friends at Briset. There was Lucy, who'd been bullied at school, and Dale, who had a load of family problems. Dale and I were at a similar place in our adolescence, both wanting to stay up all night playing computer games like *Street Fighter Alpha III*, driving Mum mad with our one-word catchphrases, like 'Safe!' Most of the time we just stared at the screens, competing with the computer handsets. We smoked a bit of dope together, but I couldn't even puff on a joint properly, having to ask Dale to blow the smoke into my mouth instead. I got a bit smashed as a result, but I wasn't that impressed. I preferred it when we got drunk on cider.

When I was alone I used to be able to lose myself when I was watching things on screens, happily immersing myself in *Alien* and Freddy Krueger movies. Freddy held my imagination tightly. He was a serial killer and child killer, who attacked his victims from inside their own dreams and nightmares. I could get that concept totally. My dreams and visions often seemed that real. Like me, Freddy was trapped in hell, 'the son of a hundred maniacs' – wicked! I lived in my own private universe.

> One, two, Freddy's coming for you.
> Three, four, better lock your door.
> Five, six, grab your crucifix.
> Seven, eight, gonna stay up late.
> Nine, ten, never sleep again.

We are all the sum total of our own experiences, and I knew all about crucifixes from Mum's God Squad adventures, and from all those early school days spent staring at statues covered in the blood of Christ. It all fitted together in my head, became part of my troubled interior world, a world I thought was a laugh, certainly a lot more of a laugh than the things that had been happening around the exterior of my world. I was looking for new heroes and mythical figures to hang my own dreams on, since any chance of becoming John Travolta in *Grease*, or Freddy Mercury, or even Billy Idol, now seemed to be receding. Not that I'd totally given up my fantasies of doing something in the music industry.

Because of all the different problems pupils at Briset had, and because there were so few of us, there was a limited number of academic subjects the staff could cover. One of the things they weren't able to do was music, which was a major disappointment. I loved music, always had done, and I was good at it. Mum had bought me a second-hand Atari when my troubles first started and I'd been composing some songs of my own, remembering all the lessons that Dave had taught me when we lived together. I was pleased with the results and it made me feel good to pour my energies into something creative. It would have been great to be able to develop it at the school as well. I still liked the idea of doing something in music, following in Mum's footsteps, even if it meant entertaining people in the streets rather than filling Wembley stadium; it's those sorts of dreams and fantasies that keep you going in the low moments.

At weekends, when I wasn't hanging out with Dale, I would stay up into the small hours of the morning composing track after track, my tics and twitches vanishing as I poured my energies through my fingers into the keyboard. My first song after I got Tourette's was called 'Angry Man'. It had a strong, pumping base, which I found comforting. I wrote another one called 'Tragedy', which used to make Mum cry when she heard it.

A couple of years later, when I was on the Internet, I came across a competition organized by BT called 'Get Out There'. They'd put together a piece of film and wanted people to write music to accompany it. The film was of this guy with his Walkman in a car park and the music invaded the man, sending his body mad, a bit tourettey really, and then he was transformed and flew out of this world. I went to work writing a track, and managed to create a whooshing sound as he went up to heaven. I submitted it and the idea then was that people coming on-line would listen to all the tracks and vote for the ones they liked the best, creating a sort of hit parade. I guess there must have been thousands of entries but mine still got into the top ten and went up as far as number two. It was amazing to see it happen, knowing all those people out there were listening to something that had come out of my own head, and were liking it. I guess that's what it's like to make a hit record and see it going up the charts, hearing it playing on the radio, watching other people enjoying it. It must be a fantastic feeling.

* * *

I was curious to know what I looked like when I was twitching and ticcing, so I set a camera up in my bedroom and filmed myself for a while. When I watched the playback I was horrified. I'd had no idea it looked that bad. I hated what I saw and didn't want to go out into the world at all, just to stay indoors or in the van on the way to and from Briset. I felt totally self-conscious and aware of what I must look like to everyone else. When you're starting out on your teen years you want to be able to control how you present yourself to the world; you want to be cool, you want to be fit, you want to be popular and you want to be normal. You don't want to be a fucking, gurning freak.

After the Tourette's had been going on for about a year Mum took me to see a homeopath for a bit of alternative healing. She was always open to new ideas and willing to try anything. I was given some powder, which I obediently took, because I was pretty sure such a tiny dose wouldn't have the same effect as the pills I'd been given in the past. Almost immediately I had a really massive spasm and then some of the symptoms started to seem a little better. The problem was I then developed a new habit. I would stand bolt upright and howl like a wolf, then I would drop to the floor in a dead faint, like those people with narcolepsy who just fall asleep wherever they are, without warning, and can't be woken up. I wouldn't have any idea it had happened, just lying there for a few moments, unconscious. Then I would come round, find myself on the floor, scramble back on to my feet, howl again and then faint again. It went on and on like that. One time it continued without a break for twenty minutes, howling and falling to the floor four times every minute. In the end I was ambulanced back into hospital.

The doctors couldn't understand it; fainting wasn't supposed to have anything to do with Tourette's. They wondered if perhaps they had been giving me too much Prozac for my depression (I was on four tablets a day at the time), and they took the dose down, which seemed to improve things. There were so many unknowns, so much uncertainty, so many possibilities in the cocktail of symptoms and medications, so much fear about what might happen next, what new horror would strike and when.

Although they didn't teach music, Briset did do art and there was a teacher called Mrs Harrison who was really brilliant and seemed to like me. She told me she thought I had real talent. Up till the explosion, it had been assumed I would do a normal range of GCSEs, go on to take A-levels and then study music or art at university, but now all those plans had been blown apart and everything I had planned for my future had changed. There was no way I could read textbooks like other people, write essays or sit through exams. But Mrs Harrison believed I could still get a qualification in art because I had enough natural talent to get me through. She refused to give up on me and fought all the way to make sure I sat the exam.

It didn't feel like there were that many people on my side beyond my family at that stage, and her encouragement meant a lot. A teacher who takes a personal interest in you can make a difference to the whole of your life. She gave me a real taste for art. I loved Salvador Dali and his surrealistic work, it's such a tripped-out style, like a snapshot of the sort of thing that goes on in my head all the time. I remade one of his pictures in my own style.

Although I felt safe at Briset, and I really liked Mrs Harrison, the rest of the staff didn't seem to know what to do with me. They were all nice but they didn't really seem to understand what Tourette's was about. One of the teachers was a bit of a sergeant major and he thought he could sort all my problems out for me with a bit of old-fashioned discipline. 'If something can be learnt,' he barked at Mum, meaning the Tourette's symptoms, 'it can be unlearnt.'

Mum tried to explain to him that I couldn't do anything about any of the tics, but he didn't believe her and started on his own campaign to teach me the error of my ways. Every time I hit myself he would look at me reprovingly and say sternly, 'You've let yourself down, Peter.' He tried to teach me to hit the table instead of my chest or throat, but he didn't understand – I wanted to relieve the tension inside me, not beat up some innocent table. The more he went on at me the more stressed I became, and the more stressed I became the more frequently I would 'let myself down'.

Other teachers reported that I 'liked distracting other students'. Liked it? Did they really believe I wanted to be constantly attracting everyone's attention? Did they truly think I was doing it by choice, seeking attention or sympathy?

'He needs to learn to control himself and calm down,' one report announced. If only I could have done exactly that all my problems would have been over in a second. If only I could have just 'pulled myself together' life would have been back to normal. Any suggestions on how I might have done that would have been gratefully received, but they didn't have any, any more than anyone else did. They suspected I was putting at least some of it on for a laugh and should make an effort to stop showing off. The local fire brigade came to give a demonstration one day and everyone was staring at me as I twisted around on the carpet in front of them, all asking me to be quiet because I was spoiling the event for everyone else.

Some of the girls at Briset were right little slappers, which was a bit of a shock to me. I liked them because they were funny and came at life from a very different angle: I just hadn't realized that there were girls my age who behaved like that. I was waiting at the bus stop for the school van with a couple of them one day when an old bloke came up and started talking to them. The girls, both of whom were fifteen, asked him if he fancied a blowjob. To my horror he agreed and they took him behind a bush to execute the deal. I was terrified they were going to be murdered and didn't know what to do. Should I go for help? What if the bus came? What would I say? The panic sent me into a touretting spin of twitching and punching.

The girls reappeared a few minutes later with the job apparently done to everyone's satisfaction and all the way back on the van they were giggling about what his cock had tasted like and waving around the ten-pound note he'd given them. It was quite funny and interesting in a way, but unsettling at the same time and I couldn't understand how they could have so little self-respect. They thought they were really cool but the event completely freaked me out and Mum could see I was in even more of a state than usual when I got home that evening. She made me tell her what had happened and I begged her not to say anything at the school.

'It's no good, Pete,' she said. 'I'll have to say something. I don't want you at a place with people like that.'

She'd been wanting to force the authorities to find somewhere more helpful for me from the beginning and saw this as her opportunity. She went in and complained, demanding I be sent somewhere more suitable. The girls found out I'd grassed on them and one of them pretended to commit suicide, letting me know it would have been all my fault if she'd died. More guilt and confusion to try to think my way through. The incident spiralled completely out of control and eventually the headmaster had to confess to Mum that she was right, Briset wasn't the right place for me. By that time I'd been there over a year without really progressing at all, but at least I'd met Mrs Harrison and got my Art GCSE.

When you have as many problems as our family did during those years, you quickly find out who your real friends are. There were so many people who were incredibly kind to us. Mum had never learnt to drive, and so whenever she got jobs she always had to find ways of getting back and forth without spending a fortune on public transport. We had friends who were endlessly generous with their time, driving us around, helping us with whatever we needed. It's impossible to explain how much the kindness of people means when you're struggling just to survive, and as a family we have always been blessed with loyal friends. Mum did learn to drive later, once I'd moved away, which was an amazing achievement. It took her three goes at the test. The first one she failed before she even got out of the test centre. I was really proud of her when she took me out in her battered little red Fiesta for the first time, despite the fact that I was clinging on to the seat for dear life.

In among all the wonderful, selfless people of the world, however, there are always the snakes who are looking for opportunities to take what they want from any situation. A sinister-looking man befriended Mum at one of her jobs and showed a very fatherly interest in me. Mum was surprised by how friendly he suddenly was towards us, especially when he turned up one day at our house with a present for me.

'Pete's upstairs in his room,' Mum told him. 'Take it on up to him while I put the kettle on.'

When he came into the room I was lying on the floor and there was something about him that I wasn't comfortable with. But the guy had come all that way to give me a present, so I wasn't going to be rude. I have a real problem with being rude to people anyway, despite the stuff that Tourette's sends out of my mouth all the time. He was acting like we were best friends, and then he got down on the floor and started to play-fight with me. Kind of odd, and a bit dangerous because my Tourette's didn't like me to be touched by anyone strange, but I gritted my teeth and succeeded in holding it in until he got me pinned to the floor, face down, yanked down the back of my pants and started smacking and rubbing my bum – definitely not cool! I wriggled and struggled to fight him off. Aware that my Tourette's was rising up inside me, I rolled on to my back to protect my bum and his hand shot down the front of my pants and grabbed the top inch of my cock. Fucking hell!

Most of the time Tourette's is the enemy, but at that moment it was my saviour. With one tremendous spasm, sending a surge of supernatural strength into my arms, I pushed him off me, amazed to see him flying through the air as if in slow motion, crashing into the wall and sliding slowly down to the floor, like a scene from a *Tom and Jerry* cartoon – SuperTouretter Strikes Again!

He looked totally panic stricken as he struggled to get back on to his feet and regain at least some of his dignity.

'We were only play fighting,' he stuttered, just to make sure I wasn't under any misapprehension that he might fancy me or something. 'Don't tell your mother anything about this. She's got enough to worry about with all your problems; this could be the thing that sends her over the edge. She could end up killing herself.'

I knew bloody well Mum would never kill herself and leave Alex and me on our own – especially over something as stupid as this, so I told her the moment I went down-stairs after our friend had beaten a hasty retreat from the house. We decided not to bother the police or anything but Mum let him know just what she thought of him, and also told any mutual friends we had, just in case he told them something different about us – wanker!

Before I left the Briset Centre the staff arranged for me to do some work experience in an office. I was sur-prised by how much I enjoyed my first experience of the ultra-straight working world. The bosses let me muck about on their computers and I designed them new busi-ness cards and some company Christmas cards, which they said they were pleased with. Everyone was incredi-bly nice to me, but whether they would ever have given me a full-time job I will never know.

Mum got me work at Music City studio as well, setting up sound stages and doing sound engineering. By that time I'd learnt to use the Cubase music programme and was writing my own music on a computer. It was interesting, and at least it showed that it was possible I would be able to find a job in the real world when the time came, but I already knew I would rather be performing on stages and in studios than setting them up. I wanted a job where I could be creative and where I could perform and entertain people. The question was, how to get there from the low point that I now found myself at. Becoming a successful performer is hard enough when you're firing on all your cylinders, but when your entire engine is fucked it begins to feel like you might be dreaming the impossible dream.

CHAPTER FOURTEEN

OBSESSION

Now that it was becoming clearer what sort of education and support I needed to help me adapt to life spent coping with Tourette's, Mum started searching for a special school that was near enough for us to get to and would help me prepare for the next step. She was saying a lot of prayers at the same time, trusting that she would receive some sort of divine guidance as to where to go next. I guess when you haven't got a partner to discuss these sorts of personal problems with, God is the next best thing. She got hold of a reference book and the first page it fell open at showed a place in Kent called Parkwood Hall School. Deciding it must be fate taking a hand, a message of some sort from on high, she rang the school and asked if they had any other pupils with Tourette's. They told her they already had four other kids with the illness. That sounded encouraging.

'Do you do independence training?' she asked, because at that stage I couldn't even leave the house without her beside me. I had to have someone there in case I went into one of my long fits on the floor of a shop or a bus or out in the street. Every outing was a nightmare for both of us. Crowds would form around us wherever I exploded, people gawping and pointing and calling me a freak.

'He's having an epileptic fit,' helpful people would say.

'No, he's not,' Mum would insist, while trying to help me at the same time as coping with Alex, who was endlessly philosophical about my embarrassing oddities. Maybe he thought everyone's big brother was the same.

'You should call an ambulance,' helpful voices in the crowd would suggest.

'There's no point,' Mum would say, over and over again. 'By the time they get here he'll be well enough to get home.'

'He shouldn't be allowed out in public,' they'd say. 'It's a disgrace.'

Taxis and bus drivers would take one look at me and would refuse to accept me as a passenger in case I did some sort of damage to their vehicles or endangered their other passengers. Once Mum took me out for a meal at a Mexican restaurant as a treat and all the other customers got up and left, not wanting to have to eat while looking at a freak like me. They were all so indignant, so affronted, as if I had deliberately set out to spoil their evenings, as if I had no right to be there because I couldn't behave appropriately. Some of the time I thought perhaps they were right, after all I didn't want to spoil anyone else's fun, and so I would hide myself away at home, not wanting to go through the embarrassment and humiliation of being rejected and reminded that I was now an outsider in society, not welcome to sit at the same table as the rest of the world. At other times, when my confidence was up a bit, I would think, fuck 'em, if I can put up with this twenty-four hours a day, every day of the year, they can put up with it for a couple of hours. They might even learn something from the experience and go away with a bit more understanding of other people, as well as having a nice meal.

The only thing I ever did on my own was get in the van to go to Briset and back; that was my life, inside the flat, inside the school or inside the van. The rest of the world was too terrifying to contemplate without Mum at my side to make everything right every time it went wrong. At an age when most boys are starting to function as adults, going out into the world, getting jobs, living away from home, trying things out, making mistakes, getting on with life, I was living more or less like a six-year-old, terrified of venturing out into an apparently hostile world, sitting in corners, shivering, my legs buckling beneath me like they had been turned to jelly. When most boys would rather die than be seen in public with their mothers, I had no choice, because I couldn't survive without her.

* * *

On top of everything else, I had developed Obsessive Compulsive Disorder as well. OCD is a neurosis that forces you to carry out repetitive, ritualized acts – all the fucking time. David Beckham recently announced that he has it, feeling compelled to make everything neat, lining cans of drink up in the fridge, that sort of thing. Gazza (Paul Gascoigne) has it as well, always having to tap on doors a certain number of times before passing through them. The condition is often linked to tidiness and cleanliness – people who like to have everything orderly and in its place around them otherwise they feel vulnerable and unsafe. Most people know someone who is a bit like that, but I wasn't just a bit like that, I was completely demented.

The worst manifestation of it for me was teeth cleaning. How simple should cleaning your teeth be? Every child usually has it mastered by the age of five, don't they? And then try to get out of doing it every opportunity they can. Not me. I would spend up to two hours in the bathroom scrubbing at my teeth and gums every morning, certain that terrible things would happen to me and I would be killed if I didn't do it exactly the right number of times in exactly the right way. I scrubbed and brushed in exactly the same sequence until my gums were bleeding and the enamel was wearing off my teeth. I would be twisting and contorting and banging around the room all the time I was brushing, the noise echoing horribly off the bare walls, but I didn't dare stop. I had to keep going, on and on and on, brushing till the blood flowed. If Mum tried to stop me I would become frantic with panic, terrified of what would happen if I didn't do it exactly right. If my teeth had been brushed in the correct way then I felt I had put a barrier up between me and the hostile world outside. I then felt strong and able to cope, like I had erected a shield around myself. If I hadn't been able to do it properly I would feel vulnerable and that would make me completely freak out.

Sometimes my obsessions would insist that I took on other rituals, like walking in a particular direction all the time, having to plan routes so I always turned left, or always turned right, whatever the orders of the day were from the OCD command centre in my brain. If I saw a particular car I would have to walk round it twice before I could go any further, or I would have to swing round a certain lamp post every time I passed it. At one time anything I saw that was yellow I had to walk round. It would take hours to just get down the street sometimes, my whole life being eaten up with hours and hours of ridiculous, meaningless, superstitious rituals. Part of me knew they were stupid, but another part forced me to obey them as if they were the biggest rules in the universe, just in case they turned out to be valid. Imagine if I stopped brushing my teeth two minutes early and was then run over by a truck outside the house, how bad would that be? Better just do those extra two minutes then, to be on the safe side.

I was convinced too that if I left the house without my hair being absolutely perfectly symmetrical something awful would happen, like I would be killed. It would take me hours of fussing and brushing to get it good enough to face the world. What had started as 'Parting Peter's' funny little ways when I was a small boy had morphed into something altogether more sinister and debilitating.

Then there was the hand washing, over and over again, determined to get rid of every last germ for fear of some dire, unspecified consequences, and the bum wiping, which made me sore from the rubbing in my attempts to get it spotlessly clean. (Which is why I like detachable showerheads so I can clean myself thoroughly down there and soothe the soreness at the same time. They didn't have one in the *Big Brother* house, which I found really difficult.)

Stupid, obsessional behaviours were taking up great chunks of every day and what time was left after that was filled with tics and spasms, swearing and howling. If I was ever going to lead an independent life away from Mum I was going to need someone to help get my confidence up and teach me some of the coping skills needed for survival. No one can go from total dependency to total independence in one move.

The people at Parkwood Hall said they would be happy to meet me, which meant Mum might be able to squeak in getting me statemented before I was too old for State help. I was just about to be sixteen and by then I'd had Tourette's for eighteen months. In that short time I had gone from being a normal, if bullied, boy to being an officially endorsed social problem.

Mum has always been one for keeping an open mind about everything, and she had started doing a thing called 'creative visualization'. Basically it means you picture what it is you want to happen, create a picture in your head which you keep concentrating on, and then you relax and the universe will make it happen for you. Fed up with living on a horrible estate where I was frightened to even stick my nose outside the door, she started to visualize a lovely three-bedroom house with trees behind it and garden all around. She drew a picture of her vision and concentrated on it hard every night before going to sleep, beaming it out into the cosmos.

She then sat back to let the universe do its work, and a few weeks later a friend came running in to tell us that there had been an announcement from the council that they were planning to knock down all the blocks of flats around us, including ours, and we would be entitled to a three-bedroom house in exchange. Does the universe operate in weird and wonderful ways or what?

We didn't initially know where we would be moved to and I was quite scared we would be moved to Eltham, close to Thomas Tallis school where all the boys who had bullied me hung out. I didn't fancy going back into their territory; it seemed like asking for trouble. They would see it as a direct challenge to their authority on the street, an affront to their rules of what was cool. They would want to crush me as quickly as a chef would want to crush a cockroach that had dared to enter his kitchen. I was so worried about it Mum rang the council and asked if they could make sure we weren't in close proximity to the school. The woman on the other end of the line said that since Mum was the only person in the whole block who hadn't asked for a house with central heating as a priority, she thought she had just the place for us.

'So it's going to be some horrible old dump then, is it?' Mum said, only half joking.

'Let's think positively, shall we, Mrs Stephenson?' the woman replied.

When they showed us the house they were offering us we couldn't believe it could actually be ours. It was a proper semi-detached house, made of bricks, with a huge back garden and trees all around. It was a beautiful place, standing in Well Hall Road, a main road, not on one of the estates that I had always found so threatening. It was also far enough from Thomas Tallis for me to feel safe. Mum had noticed there were a lot of CCTV cameras in the road, so she thought that would protect me a bit more when I was out. It fulfilled all our dreams and we accepted it happily.

It wasn't till we had moved in that we began to find out more about Well Hall Road. The house was almost opposite the bus stop where Stephen Lawrence had been murdered in 1993. Stephen, an eighteen-year-old guy who was planning to become an architect, had been going home at about 10.30 at night with a friend and had needed to change buses. He'd got off one in Well Hall Road and crossed over to see if another was coming. A group of white youths spotted him, shouted out some sort of abuse and then, in the words of a witness, 'engulfed him', stabbing him several times, pushing the knife five inches into his chest, punishing him just because he was black and had dared to come on to their patch. He managed to get away and staggered a hundred yards down the road before his strength finally bled away and he fell. He was dead before he reached the hospital.

It was a shocking crime because it was so senseless, a mindless lynching of an ordinary, decent young guy. It was an area filled with the same right-wing spite and hate that I had experienced as a small child out walking with my Indian childminder's children. Anyone who was different, either because of the colour of their skin or because they walked around ticcing and swearing, was liable to end up in trouble. It was a cruel, intolerant place, full of hatred and menace. People were suspicious of anyone who didn't conform, didn't have the same clothes and the same haircut as them. Anyone who tried to be different or tried to achieve something better had to be abused and attacked, cut down to size, reminded who was in charge. It was a giant version of the worst school playgrounds I had experienced.

Mum was on her hands and knees outside the front door one day, planting some bulbs, when two shirtless thugs came meandering past on the communal grass, apparently indifferent to her presence.

'Yeah,' one of them boasted to his friend, nodding towards the bus stop, 'it felt fucking great when I stuck the knife in.'

Mum plucked up the courage to ring the police and tell them, and two and a half years later an officer came round to ask her about the incident, by which time it seemed a little late.

There was a plaque set into the pavement in memory of Stephen, but passers-by would spit on it, so they had to have a CCTV camera trained on it day and night. That was what life in Well Hall Road was like.

I knew that I wouldn't have to stay at the house all that much if Parkwood would be willing to accept me as a pupil because I would be able to board there full time. We were taken to see it the first time by a big black guy called Brian, who turned out to be my carer when I got there. I immediately felt comfortable and at home with him. In fact I liked just about everything about the place. It was out in the countryside and had its own little farm with sheep and goats. They said they would love to have me and they could work out a plan for the next two years of my life. I thought it would be a really cool place to be. I would be living there most of the time, which would give Mum and Alex a bit of space, and it would get me used to the idea of managing without them. It was owned by the Royal Borough of Kensington and Chelsea, so all we had to do was persuade them to come up with the £30,000 grant needed to fund me for those two years. Mum revved up everyone in the church in Peckham to pray for me and pulled every string she could think of. She's a wicked letter writer when she's got a cause to get her teeth into.

Ever since my problems had started we always seemed to be waiting for something or someone, for a phone call or for someone to raise our case at a meeting, or for someone to say yes to a request for help. When you have a problem that you can't solve yourself, you immediately fall into the power of others and it some-times feels as if some of them take pleasure in making you suffer as much as possible, building the suspense like second-rate game show hosts. The people who held my fate in their hands were having their last meeting at six o'clock one evening and they still hadn't received the necessary paperwork from Greenwich. I thought Mum was going to blow a fuse. She rang her MP, who stuck his oar in at the last moment and finally the vibe got through to the right places, the right papers got to the right people and I was cleared to go.

There were some people at Parkwood who were a lot worse off than me and only a couple of guys I could really talk to at any length. There were some Down's syndrome guys who were really friendly, some guys with various degrees of autism and others who had an illness that made them eat everything they came across until eventually they just keeled over. And I thought I had problems? The other guys with Tourette's seemed to be having more trouble than me coming to terms with the problem. They had real difficulty keeping cheerful. They were all really cool, but it was hard to find people to have a conversation with. I spent a lot of my time with Brian, the carer. He became like my best friend in the place.

I find that having a condition like mine heightens my sensitivities towards other people with problems. I've discovered that I can always tell when there is another Tourette's sufferer nearby, even before they make a giveaway movement or noise. It's like the Tourette's version of 'Gaydar', I can just sense their vibe in the air.

The school authorities wanted to assess me quite soon after I got there, to work out exactly what they were dealing with, so they put me in a room full of inspectors with pads and pencils. I was sitting in the middle, getting myself prepared to be studied, and they were all sitting round me in a circle. They were all firing questions from different angles and the pressure started building up in my head. I find answering questions difficult. I can't always locate the answers when I want to. I know they're in my head somewhere, but just not to hand. I start rummaging frantically in my internal filing systems and then I worry that I'm letting people down by not being able to give them what they want as quickly as I should.

Then they were talking about me among themselves, while I just sat there and the pressure kept building inside me to get something out. I held on and held on until I couldn't bear the strain any longer and had to blurt it out.

'Wankers, all of yer!'

That, unfortunately, seemed to win back their attention.

It was the first time I'd used that phrase, or even that word, but from that moment on I couldn't stop it. The needle was stuck and there was nothing I could do to change it. It was goodbye to 'Bollocks' and hello to 'Wankers, all of yer!'

It wasn't just the words themselves that were the problem; it was the tone of voice that they came out with. It was an aggressive, angry, ugly voice which made the phrase sound as if the insult was directed personally at whoever was within earshot. It was personal and specific, and therefore threatening and offensive. Imagine yourself walking into a pub full of people you don't know, going up to the bar and shouting, 'Wankers, all of yer' at the locals. Some people will simply look shocked and move away, feeling under attack, I guess, embarrassed, unsure how to respond.

But others will automatically retaliate in the same aggressive tone.

'Who you calling a wanker?'

It would usually be no good me trying to explain that I wasn't actually talking to them, or to anyone else for that matter, but rather to the world in general, because the more I would stumble to get the explanations out the more expletives would come tumbling out with them, making the situation worse and worse, digging the hole deeper and deeper until I could no longer see over the sides. In most cases it was better to just turn round and leg it. I did a lot of running away from angry blokes in those years.

Just when I thought it couldn't get any worse, 'cunt' started popping out all over the place. Some people might find 'shit', 'bollocks' and 'wanker' funny, they may even have grown used to hearing 'fuck' since everyone started using it on television, but 'cunt' is a whole other thing. There are still a lot of people who will say that it is the one word they can't stand, particularly women, and there I was spraying it around like it meant nothing worse than 'Have a nice day'. A fucking disaster!

There was nothing I could do about it. Once my mouth had started on it, it wasn't going to let go. It's surprising how a word loses its power when you hear it every couple of minutes. Before long it was just another sound to me and to the people who were with me all the time, but there was no mistaking the power to offend that it still held when it reached the ears of others who weren't used to it or expecting it.

Sometimes when a new word made its way into my daily vocabulary, it would push another one out. 'Bollocks' has more or less gone now, and a straight 'Wankers' eventually replaced 'Wankers, all of yer!' thank God. But then the current words begin to morph and join up and make new phrases, so I was soon stuck with 'cuntywanks', which Dickie in *Big Brother* decided was his favourite. I know not many people would agree with him there.

For every step forward, I seemed doomed to take two steps back.

CHAPTER FIFTEEN

DRESSING UP

When I got to eighteen I was allowed to share a cottage in the grounds of Parkwood Hall with some of the other guys. It was a bit like the *Big Brother* house in a way. We had our own iron, washing machine and dryer and we were learning how real life worked for people who didn't intend to live with their mothers for the rest of their lives. They were all nice guys but I was beginning to feel ready to move on, back into the real world, to look for a bit more mental stimulation, a bit more creativity. It didn't seem likely that my Tourette's was going to get any better, so what was the point in putting off the day when I and the rest of the world had to face each other?

They didn't do much academic education at Parkwood for someone of my age. I really wanted to keep my art going, so they said I could go on day release to a nearby mainstream school called Hextable to do an art A-level. I was nervous at the thought of returning to a mainstream school, worried about the reaction I would get, but it turned out to be totally cool. Maybe my Tourette's was better when I was there because I was distracted by the art. Maybe my peer group had matured since I left Thomas Tallis, or maybe it was because they were all artists and therefore cooler about things like weirdness. Or maybe they were just nicer people. Whatever the reason it was great to mix with others who liked art as much as I did, who talked the same language, laughed at the same things and seemed to like me despite the fact that I was different.

I hadn't lost the knack of drawing and painting; if anything Tourette's had stimulated my talent, giving it an extra charge of energy and imagination, and I ended up getting an A grade, which made me very proud and very grateful to the school. It felt great to show that I could still achieve stuff, even when my whole body was in open revolt against me, even when every other subject on the curriculum had become an impossible obstacle course.

I created a gory painting of myself with my chest ripped open and someone else inside looking sad and violent, like the tourettey alien who lives inside me, squatting uninvited, making endless mischief for the host body. In another picture my whole body was contorted and stretched out on a bed of bloodied nails. The school have kept it on the wall even after all this time, which makes me feel happy.

Now and then I would get commissioned to do a piece by someone as well, actually getting paid, which made me wonder if perhaps I could make a full-time career from it. On Jimmy Somerville's fortieth birthday I was commissioned by a friend to do a portrait of him. I painted it in two parts, with Jimmy in hell with horns on one side and in paradise with a halo on the other, with the snake from the Garden of Eden coming out of an arsehole in the corner. I was pleased with the result, especially as Jimmy seemed to like it.

At Hextable I had another girlfriend, the first since the explosion had rocked my self-confidence. She was a nice girl, good fun, but not someone to go 'all the way' with.

'If you love me,' she said for a laugh one day when we were alone together, 'you'll let me make you up.'

'Yeah, all right then,' I said, enjoying the idea, always up for anything like that. All my life I've loved dressing up and face painting and stuff like that, so I sat back and let her do her thing, enjoying the attention and the physical closeness as she concentrated on making me beautiful. She gave me the full works – lippy, eyes, everything. I liked the sensual feel of the paint being stroked on to my face and the scent of the cosmetics in my nostrils, a comforting, girly, showbizzy smell.

'Wow, man!' When I looked in the mirror I really liked what I saw staring back. 'Amazing. That's wicked. I love it. I'm gonna keep that.'

So I did, but that was the end of the relationship because she thought that meant I was gay or something. I didn't get the connection myself. I know some guys in their teens get a bit confused about their sexuality but it never bothered me. Perhaps it was because I'd been accused of being gay from such an early age I had given the question more thought than some people and real-ized that it just wasn't me. Maybe it was because I had known so many cool gay guys when I was a kid. Maybe I should just have gone all the way with her to prove something, but then, who needs to prove stuff? I'd been around gay blokes all my life, from Poofy-Cousin-Marcus to Jimmy Somerville and Marc Almond and I knew I didn't have any inclinations that way. That didn't mean I didn't think their lifestyle choices weren't cool, though. Yeah, make-up for blokes, why not? Wicked!

I didn't bother with the lipstick, just the eye shadow and eyeliner and nail varnish. Mum didn't even blink. She thought it looked good, but then she'd grown up in the era of Punks and New Romantics, hung out with all the gay groups, seen the rise of Boy George and Adam Ant. She thought the look suited me and so did I. Maybe it reminded her of what Dad looked like when she first met him nearly twenty years before.

As soon as my new girlfriend dumped me I went for the full New Romantic look, wearing lots of lace, Mum's shiny velvet tops, leopard scarves, lacy gloves and glit-tery brooches. I used to raid Mum's drawers when I was little because she had so much cool stuff from her punk period and her hippy period that I could use for dressing up, now it all fitted better. Mum encouraged me because it was a look she had always liked herself. She gave me a velvet vampire cape and leather trousers for Christmas. 'I am the dandy highwayman' – wicked!

I started to buy most of my own stuff in charity shops and boot sales, hunting out the best pieces from among the dross. I've always liked to strut around in front of the mirror, wear dramatic clothes, create a look, make an impact. It's all part of the theatre of life, bringing a little colour and drama to our everyday world. We all need a bit of cheering up now and then, don't we?

Now that I was finding myself accepted for who I was at Parkwood and Hextable, I was beginning to get used to the idea that I was different, and beginning to enjoy it in some ways. Part of that being different was deliberate, with the clothes and make-up, and part was most definitely not deliberate. But I was coming to realize that the Tourette's was as much part of who I was as my hairstyle or my eyeballs.

People were going to stare at me in the street anyway, so I might as well dress like I wanted to, look nice in my own way, feel good about myself when I looked in the mirror. It might make me more of a target for the bullies and homophobes, but they already had me in their sights anyway, so, fuck it, let's go for it and risk the consequences.

I got myself a bike to speed up my journeys around Eltham when I went home in the hope that I could pedal faster than my tormentors could run. Groups of girls would point and laugh and shout out as I cycled past, scarves blowing in the wind behind me. I didn't mind that sort of laughter so much, although I was always aware that it could tip over into aggression and violence at any moment, particularly if I was on trains and buses, where I would be trapped and unable to escape if things turned nasty. I knew to stay away from places like that, to always leave myself with an escape route; survival tactics for life in the jungle.

The swear words that Tourette's pops into my mouth every few sentences would be hurled at me from passing cars, open windows and street corners wherever I went, as if the whole area wanted to make sure I was aware that I was a freak and they didn't like me. That aspect was horrible, but I knew that if I wanted to have any sort of life at all I had to brazen it out, otherwise they would have succeeded in making me into something I wasn't, would have forced me to suppress my real personality and live a lie. This was who I was and if I dressed any differently I would be lying to myself as well as to the rest of the world. Somewhere deep inside I knew I had to find the courage to be out in the world as myself, bold and unapologetic, regardless of what might happen.

* * *

It was while I was at Parkwood that I realized that along with all the other gifts it had bestowed upon me, puberty had crafted me a massive knob. Other people noticed it first in the showers.

'Fucking hell, Pete,' they said, staring at it in open-gobbed amazement. 'What's going on there?'

'Dunno, mate,' I said, looking down at this new arrival, comparing it to the little things dangling between all of their legs, wondering if this was going to prove an asset or a liability.

The doctors had me on a bit of medication while I was at Parkwood to try to calm me down, but not too much or I wouldn't have been able to draw and paint. The school had a steel band as well and I was able to play on the drums, so I was getting a bit of the music back. Not that it was ever far away as the 'beat box' was always going in my head, and the Tourette's often made me vocalize the beat, drumming with my tongue or fingers or anything that would create the sounds that my body craved. It was great to be able to actually let the energy and the rhythm out on a real drum, channelling the noises out of my head. As long as my energies were being soaked up like that the Tourette's was willing to sit quietly and wait until I'd finished – surprisingly polite of it really, considering what its manners were usually like.

There was a village near to the school, which we would go out to in order to get used to being in the real world, coping with the reactions of real people. It was like a long, slow confidence-building exercise.

The teachers taught me to write everything down in a diary, because the ADD meant I could never remember anything and was always missing appointments and forgetting important things. It was a really helpful tip, giving me a bit of a handle on what was going on, putting some shape into my day and my thoughts.

Once I was away from Thomas Tallis I was never totally trapped in a bullying environment again, but I still had the odd problems in places like pubs with people taking the piss. The best plan was always to find somewhere nice and out of the way to sit and if things got ugly to just walk away. Coping mechanisms, the experts call it. Fucking survival techniques, more like.

I was feeling good, and just about ready to dive in the deep end and submerge myself back into that wonderful thing called life! Now things were going to get *really* interesting.

CHAPTER SIXTEEN

FALLING IN LOVE

Armed with my one A grade A-level, my portfolio of work, and a gently blossoming self-confidence thanks to Parkwood, Mum and a selection of good friends, I managed to get accepted at Camberwell College of Art in South London for their foundation course. It's a brilliant college and has turned out loads of interesting people over the years. Syd Barrett, the genius who started Pink Floyd and then became an infamous and barmy recluse, went there, and Laurence Llewelyn-Bowen, the decorator off the telly who dresses like a dandy, and Tim Roth, the actor who was in *Pulp Fiction* and played 'Mr Orange' in *Reservoir Dogs*. Art school's a good place to go to if you like dressing up and wearing make-up and being a bit different: everyone's open to things that are new and imaginative and fun. Everyone's ready to experiment and have a laugh.

Not all the art schools I applied to were quite so welcoming. One of the interviewers took one look at me and suggested I go back to school to get the requisite five

GCSEs. It was a strange attitude for someone from the art world to take to life. It seemed to me that talent was what should matter, not proof of a childhood spent gaining exam results. Mum got a bit agitated with this man, trying to explain that I'd spent the last three years in and out of hospitals and special schools, but he wasn't having any of it. Maybe he thought I was just trying it on, like the social worker who wouldn't give us a ground floor flat. Maybe he didn't quite understand what Tourette's can do to your life. I reckon Van Gogh would've had trouble getting in there if he hadn't had his GCSE certificates in his back pocket. Come to think of it, poor old Van Gogh probably did know a thing or two about having to deal with people like that.

Camberwell was great, full of artists and nutters. I was able to get all sorts of stuff out of my system. I made an animated 'monkey-face' out of coat hangers as one of my pieces, exorcising some old demons. I wanted to earn some money where I could, just to survive and take the strain off Mum a bit, so I started handing out fliers around the Camden Town area in my spare time. Camden's a fantastic area for people like me, full of students and people running esoteric market stalls, a Bohemian, happy place where alternative lifestyles are the norm and a bit of pantomime in the street goes down well with most people. Even there it could sometimes be a bit tricky as I was still shouting 'Wankers, all of yer!' pretty frequently, which some people took exception to. I often had to do a runner if someone took it personally and I didn't have time to defuse the situation. If you shout a phrase like that into someone's face with full force the chances are they aren't going to warm to you.

'You trying to be funny, mate?'

'Who you talking to?'

Time to go again.

The best thing about the course at Camberwell was that I met a student called Jenny. She was pretty, with beautiful waist-long hair, and I fancied her immediately. I also really liked her as a friend. The night we got together we had put on a fashion show at the school, wearing clothes we'd designed and made ourselves. I'd made a silver suit and coloured my hair and everything else to match; she was wearing a dress she had based on an orgasm, covered in words like 'lust' and 'throb'. Jenny talked about sex all the time, fascinated by it and by its place in art. It was a brilliant night, really exciting and glamorous. We were high from the adrenaline of modelling on the catwalk, strutting our stuff. That night was the first time we made love properly and from that moment I was totally in love. She really made me laugh, made me happy.

There had been another girl I'd fallen for when I first got to Camberwell. I'd been really excited when she said she would phone me on New Year's Eve, sitting around nervously waiting for the call. When it came at about nine in the evening it was actually to dump me, which was a real downer. My heart had been badly bruised from the blow, but getting together with Jenny mended everything and made me forget anyone I had ever been hurt by before. I had never had a relationship like this. My Tourette's never seemed to bother her at all, it was just part of me as far as she was concerned. Some people didn't seem to notice it at all once they got to know me; they seemed to be able to see and like me for what I was saying, not the way I was saying it.

Jenny was fabulous in every way and really talented, making films, playing the cello; she seemed to be able to do everything. She was obsessed with going round galleries, always wanting to take me with her to see more and more art. It felt like she wanted to see everything in the world. I enjoyed it almost as much as she did at first, because I wanted to be with her whatever she was doing and wherever she was going, but even when you love art you can still have enough of looking at rows and rows of pictures, at least I can. Art should be more integrated into life than that; it should catch you by surprise and please you as you go about your everyday business. It should be happening on street corners, in pubs and clubs, on pavements and in people's front rooms. Walking through hushed, church-like halls, gazing at picture after picture, all reverentially hung and lit as if they are sacred objects, is something else. It's not real life. Having said that, Mum used to like taking me to museums and things when I was tiny. She was particularly into Egyptology at one stage, Tutankhamun and all that. They provided good free entertainment and I'm sure lots of stuff seeped into my subconscious in those years, contributing to whatever came back out again in my own art later. Anything that stimulates you to have ideas and thoughts must be good.

While I was on the course at Camberwell I went on a group trip to New York. I had to get special permission from the American Embassy to be allowed on a plane with Tourette's. I suppose they thought I might frighten the other passengers, or run amok in the aisles.

I got bored shitless going round galleries with the others and wanted to get a taste of the real Manhattan, so I struck out on my own to do some exploring as soon as I could escape. I preferred to just wander the streets without a plan or an itinerary, taking any turning that looked interesting, watching the break-dancers and street entertainers, drifting round the shops, seeing the real world of the real New Yorkers, getting the vibe off the street. My Tourette's went into overdrive after all the stress of travelling, being cooped up in the plane for so long, being channelled through airports with all the dis- tractions and pressures, and then finding myself in a strange place with no idea where anything was or should be. Exhausted from the flying, and ticcing like a maniac, I got lost in the bustling, unfamiliar streets and eventually felt an overwhelming urge to sleep. Whenever I get really tired, sleep comes over me like a tidal wave and I go out almost instantly. I suppose it's because the Tourette's is living off my body like a sort of parasite, draining the electricity like the cowboy wires you see piggy-backing off the mains cables in third world cities, attached by people too poor to be able to pay for their power in the normal way. During my waking hours my internal generator has to run me and my Tourette's, and the effort takes its toll of my energy supplies.

Needing to urgently recharge my batteries, I found a grating blowing up hot air from the bowels of a skyscraper. I curled up in the warmth and immediately fell asleep like any sidewalk tramp might do, becoming part of the city in a way I never would have done while sightseeing in art galleries.

Wherever I am in the world, I always feel an overwhelming urge to interact with the environment around me, to touch things, tap them, stroke their surfaces, incorporate them into some sort of little performance. I don't know if the urge is part of the Tourette's or the ADD or the OCD or just part of me, the same little boy who wanted to show off as Freddy Mercury at his mother's wedding, who wanted to cuddle the pit bull terrier and play with the buttons in Dave's studio. If I see a statue with a finger pointing out I can't stop myself from pressing my nose to the tip of the finger and pulling a face. If I see a fountain I can't resist posing in front of it so that it looks like the water is spouting out of my mouth. There's something comforting about being in touch with everything and something urgent about the need to perform and clown at every opportunity. Maybe it's a form of attention seeking, but I don't particularly want to be the centre of attention if I'm not actually performing in some way. If I am sitting with a group of people I am often happier to be the quiet one, letting everyone else do the talking for me, conserving my energy, listening to what they have to say, learning new stuff, taking some time alone in my head.

But being in New York was like being on a movie set and I felt a strong urge to act weird. I ran around town with my pants on my head, without having any idea why. Everyone seemed to be laughing, as if they understood the urges that drove me. It was a nice vibe, a different slant on the 'Englishman in New York' thing.

When I landed back at Heathrow I decided to go round to a friend's house and ended up staying a few days, sleeping off the jet lag. Trouble was, I'd forgotten to tell Mum, who was expecting me back home, about the change of plan. This short taste of being an independent adult had made me forget I was still a worry to her and should be doing all I could to keep her mind at rest. It would only have taken one phone call, but I didn't get round to it. She became frantic with worry when she didn't hear from me and even rang the police, while I slept blissfully through the whole thing on my mate's couch.

* * *

At the end of our foundation year Jenny got accepted on to a fine arts degree course at Oxford, and I got accepted into Brighton University to study Visual and Performing Arts. There was no chance Oxford was going to take me with just one A-level and one GCSE, and Jenny was never going to pass up on the chance to go there. The thought of being separated from her broke my heart but I realized we were going to have to be apart and have other experiences for a few years. We both knew that. In a way I was looking forward to new adventures, even though I knew the separation was going to be painful, but in my heart I was telling myself it would only be temporary, that we were destined to be together forever. We spent virtually the whole of the last summer together, preparing ourselves for the agony of being temporarily separated.

When she told me she had met someone else almost the moment she got to Oxford I thought my whole world had caved in on top of me. The feelings were so strong I was frightened they would overwhelm me. The night she dumped me I went out clubbing by myself in Brighton, not able to bear the thought of being alone with my thoughts and my misery. I'd never wanted to do drugs before, never really thought about it, but that night I thought, fuck it, I might as well have some fun. I needed something to deaden the pain and distract my mind. The reality of life without Jenny at that moment was more than I could handle. I suppose I fell in love with drugs on the rebound really. They were kind to me and took me away from the pain to wonderful places in distant corners of my mind.

It took me a lot longer to get over Jenny than it had taken her to get over me. I'm not sure that I ever will be over her completely. Do people ever get over their first big loves? We're still best friends, but that's not the same thing as the feeling of being with your first love, believing that she is also going to be your last.

It's all part of growing up, isn't it? One of the shit parts.

Having had a bit of an extended childhood in some ways, allowed to be a bit of a Peter Pan, I was about to do some very fast growing up indeed.

CHAPTER SEVENTEEN

BRIGHTON

Mum was able to ring a few people she knew from her time at the university in Brighton, and I arrived in town with a ready-made set of friends and supporters to start me off. I'm always contented when I'm doing anything creative, particularly art and music. When I'm concentrating on work I feel that everything is right in my world, that my brain and my body are working together as a team, that things are as they should be in the universe. I loved all the practical work of the course and was able to pour all my thoughts and emotions into it, distracting my Tourette's and bringing the tics and twitches down to a manageable level.

I wasn't quite so comfortable with the part of the undergraduate social scene I found myself in. I was sharing with fashion students in university halls to start with, which was another '*Big Brother* without the cameras' experience, but not as benign as the Parkwood experience had been. No one picked on me or tried to bully me like they had at school, but everyone clashed about all sorts of trivial crap that I just couldn't get my head round. I was surprised by how conformist and small-minded they could be considering they were supposed to be artists. They were obsessed with the conforming side of fashion and intolerant of anything that was a bit different, out of their experience or unfashionable. They didn't seem to want to change anything or experiment with anything; they just wanted to follow the latest trends. I think fashion is great when it is all about imagination, about challenging the norm and being bold and different, but it's suffocating and horrible when it is about conforming and following some elite set of rules, excluding people who are deemed 'unfashionable'.

They all seemed a bit straight, travelling along their chosen career paths, taking no risks and doing no exploring of life around them. I wanted to sink myself into a few adventures and have as much fun as I could possibly cram into every hour I was awake. I wanted to party! Brighton seemed to me to be a city of infinite possibilities, and I was afraid I was going to miss them if I spent all my time hanging out with fellow students, bickering about whose turn it was to do the washing up. I wanted a bit of madness and in the end we all fell out and I went my separate way.

Brighton had everything I could ever have wanted from a city, from the magical, ornate, Aladdin-like domes of the Prince Regent's Palace, to the gaudy, glittering, kiss-me-quick lights of the pier. From the alternative characters who hung out in the North Laines, in the hippy, punk and goth shops and restaurants, or just sitting around on the streets, to the gays who had colonized Kemp Town, gradually transforming it from its dangerous, seedy past into something altogether more chic and camp. Everywhere there were clubs to cater for every type and every taste. Young people filled the streets at night, mixing with dropouts and dole queue musicians, and over the whole mix was spread the holiday atmosphere of a good old-fashioned seaside resort.

Local resident Fat Boy Slim could throw a party on the beach and a quarter of a million people would turn up with hardly anyone turning a hair. Thousands would go clubbing every night of the week, tens of thousands at weekends. Theatres and comedy clubs, music concerts, arts festivals and gay pride marches; things were happening every day. Street entertainers, *Big Issue* salesmen, beggars, winos, drag acts and media trendies staying in fancy boutique hotels; the whole world had come to play on the streets and on the beach, mixing and mingling and getting on with each other like they were all at one giant party. There were no uniforms, no predominant culture forcing out everyone else. Brighton fitted me like a tight leather glove.

I was still devastated over losing Jenny and trying to find ways to cheer myself up and the city provided unlimited opportunities and choices. There were lots of drugs on offer in the clubs and I was happy to have a go at any of them. People were happy to share whatever they had and if they offered me a new experience I would think, OK, why not?

Some substances were more fun than others. Smoking dope never seemed to help much, right from the days when I used to try it with Dale, just making me paranoid. The first night I set out to forget my broken heart I took three Ecstasy tablets in a psychedelic trance club, with fantastically trippy results. I was rolling around, just laughing at my own name. Club life is fabulous, so different to the underlying feeling of aggression that so often seems to simmer in pubs and bars, just waiting for an imagined insult, a misdirected look, or any other excuse to erupt into pointless violence. Everyone I met at the clubs was so welcoming, so friendly, so happy, so funny and so high. They all seemed to like me, not caring if I twitched or swore, shouted obscenities or leapt about like a lunatic in women's clothes. Why would they care? They were all just as mad in their own ways, some of them a lot madder. They were out for nights of fun and entertainment and I could provide them with plenty of those; fun was my speciality!

Once I'd started to meet a few people I got more invitations to other places and I moved into the party scene big time, my whole social life snowballing wildly.

I was doing acid, loving the colours I saw, loving the techno music, loving the dancing, loving life.

When I discovered psychedelic trance clubs and field raves I was amazed that such places could have ever existed without me knowing about them. It was like walking through a hidden door into a secret parallel world. My education started with a night at 'Escape from Samsara', an underground trance all-nighter in Brixton, packed with hippies and other cool dudes. There, in the heat and beat of the dance floor, I met a gay probation officer who instantly became a really close friend. He led me deeper into the music and gay scenes in Brighton. It was wicked! I started going to tranny parties at places like Wild Fruit, and met famous local drag acts like Mrs Ray, Mrs Joyride and Stephanie Starlet.

Having been brought up around people like Poofy-Cousin-Marcus, Jimmy Somerville, Marc Almond and Lizzie-Anne, I felt at home immediately, totally comfortable, totally unthreatened, as if I was among my own people, back in the bosom of my family. Wild Fruit was a fucking brilliant gay club, by the same people who organized things like the Alternative Miss Brighton pageant. One year they set up a four thousand capacity dance tent at the Gay Pride Festival and everyone partied the night away. Imagine: four thousand people off their heads and happy in one tent.

I loved the way trannys knew how to party, forgetting all the cares and difficulties of their everyday lives, all the prejudice and unhappiness they must have faced as they tried to find themselves and escape from their backgrounds. They always seemed to be dedicating themselves to living life to the full, refusing to be sad when there was music and laughter and drink and drugs and dancing and sex to be had. I became Mrs Ray's sidekick for a while. I just loved hanging out with her; cuddling up to her like she was my mum or a favourite aunt. Some people you just feel instantly comfortable with, regardless of what they look like or what they do for kicks.

I'd always longed to find really hard dance music, to be able to lose myself completely in a rushing, thudding, brain-jarring beat, and I had begun to wonder if the ultimate experience actually existed. But here it was, night after night. I couldn't believe that I had found exactly what I wanted. Psychedelic trance is electronic music with a really fast tempo, anything up to a hundred and fifty beats per minute. It pushed deep into my head, pumping out the endorphins, forcing me to feel fantastic, lifting me out of myself.

I would be up on stages in clubs dancing like a wild man for hours, or out in the countryside at spontaneously organized illegal raves with bonfires burning in the night skies and scraggy-looking dogs wandering among the celebrating crowd, scavenging for scraps. My Romany blood boiled up merrily in my veins.

Other people saw the way I moved, propelled by the beat of the music, by the Tourette's and by whatever substances I might have been imbibing, and they enjoyed what they saw. When you have been a freak and have grown used to people mocking you; when you have suffered a long campaign of humiliation and come out the other side, you lose all pointless inhibitions. You have nothing left to lose. I no longer cared what other people thought of me, and because I didn't care they didn't care either and accepted me for what I was.

I was a natural at the whole party animal thing and I could see that made the people around me feel good. Fun is contagious when you're among people who are up for it, who have no hang-ups, who just want to party. Club owners liked the vibe I brought with me and would ask me to perform for the crowds, leading the fun. I loved every moment of it, just like my moments as Freddy Mercury or the genie, like my puppet shows for Alex or my radio shows with Sarah. This was my element, where I was meant to be. I was in a new universe that felt completely right, flying free, mentally and physically, and feeling completely happy.

I had never known a feeling like it, and sometimes people were actually willing to pay me for doing it – for simply being Pete! I discovered that with acid I could heighten the whole experience even further, dancing all night and way past sunrise. At the outdoor parties it was the best sensation ever to be dancing in the sun to a beat that made every part of me tingle with pleasure, in the midst of all my friends. Wow, man!

I knew that adding drugs into the mix was dangerous and eventually I stopped doing much acid, preferring to get a natural high from the music and the
dancing and the happiness, even though I missed the
pretty colours. I was never tempted by heroin. I never
liked the idea of ending up a smackhead. I'd seen too
many of them and hadn't liked what I saw. But there
were other substances out there for me to try before I
felt I had explored every corner of my brain and every
dimension of my universe.

I was on a roll, flying higher and higher, feeling that
nothing could stop me now.

PERFECT PETE

I only lasted a year at the university, just like Mum, but for different reasons. Although the art and the music and performing were great, I still couldn't manage the essays and other paperwork to anything like a high enough standard. The Tourette's was not willing to give me any let-up when it came to trying to work with words. It would let me draw and it would let me paint and write music and dance, but when it came to words it drew the line. I would stare at a page and the words would fly all over the place, making my head ache with the effort of trying to pin them down and force some sense out of them. My attention wouldn't do as I told it, wandering off like a disobedient, hopelessly curious child every few seconds. I would practically burst a blood vessel trying to concentrate for the lengths of time needed to write an essay, but it was impossible, as hopeless as trying to make a hyperactive wild monkey sit down at a tea table and make polite conversation about the weather.

You can't get a degree without being able to string a few written words together in a reasonable order, or without spending a lot of time reading and researching into the subject. So it was time to accept I'd learnt all I could from the course and that it was time to move on. It wasn't such a hard decision because now I knew exactly where I wanted my life to go; I wanted to submerge myself in the other side of my life – the friends, the partying, the clubs, the music, the street life of Brighton, the city that now seemed like it had always been my spiritual home, the nirvana I had been dreaming of reaching for so long and had now discovered. My Shangri-la by the sea.

Mum had told me I would love Brighton, that once I got there everyone would accept me and it would be nothing like living in Eltham, and she was right. It was like arriving in heaven. Everyone seemed to fancy me and no one cared that I was weird. Completely the opposite in fact: they actually seemed to like me for it, applaud me, egg me on to ever weirder heights. They started called me Perfect Pete. Everybody wanted to be my friend, encouraged me to be more myself, to keep the show on the road.

I liked feeling attractive, although sometimes the attention could be so intense it would be a bit scary. I got a job in the cloakroom of a club on the beach called Concorde 2, which meant I was often walking home across the city late at night, when the streets were less crowded. One night this guy started following me in a car.

'Let me suck your cock!' he shouted.

Aware there was no one else around, and suddenly feeling vulnerable, I declined the offer, but he wasn't going to be put off that easily. He kept tailing me, going on and on, his tone growing more threatening with every refusal. If he couldn't tempt me into it with charm he was going to try to bully me into it. I felt my heartbeat quicken, like being back in the playground, remembering the moments when my instincts would warn me that the tide of sympathy was turning against me, that they wanted to hurt me, punish me. Sensing imminent danger I speeded up my pace but still the car was on my tail, the increasingly abusive voice pursuing me. In the end I ran for my life, diving into side roads to escape. I nearly shat my pants.

Usually the attention I received wasn't frightening at all, just funny and flattering and interesting. If someone gay hit on me I would just have to tell them I was straight and they would be fine about it, shrugging their regrets and moving on to their next target of the night. Some straight men are so paranoid they are going to be raped or something the moment a gay man even looks at them. I don't know why, maybe they've watched *Deliverance* a few times too many. Most gays wouldn't hurt a fly, quite the opposite. I guess girls must get the same attention from heterosexual men all the time and they have to learn to deal with it.

I loved going to the gay clubs and drag nights because it was a chance to dress up and, like the trannys, gays always have so much fun at parties. I went to one Halloween party at the Perfumed Gardens, a gay techno music club, dressed as Little Miss Perfect (Perfect Pete's fun-loving baby sister, I guess), dropped some acid and had a really great night. Imagine even thinking of trying to do that in Eltham; I would have been lying in a pool of blood on the pavement before I even got two feet from my own front door.

One night a gay guy stopped me in the street and told me how he'd had a row with his boyfriend (I think his boyfriend had been unfaithful or something), and he wanted to take home another man's pants to throw in his face and make him jealous. It sounded like a pretty logical thing to do at the time.

'Can I buy your pants off you for twenty quid?' he asked.

I thought I would be overcharging him at that price.

'Don't worry, mate,' I said. 'You can have them for a tenner.'

He accepted the offer, I dropped them, handed them over and he ran off with them over his head, happy as anything. Shit like that cheers the day up.

Another guy approached me during another night out in the Perfumed Gardens, and told me I was gorgeous.

'Really?' I was always pleased to hear it.

DANCING ANGEL AT THE
PERFUME GARDENS, BRIGHTON,
AGED 20.

AT THE TORTURE GARDENS WITH GIL,
SUMMER '02.

IN DRAG, HAVING MY TITS GROPED BY A SKELETON BEFORE I WAS EATEN
BY A ZOMBIE.

BELOW: ME, JOOLZ AND CHERRY.

WITH MY MATES CRAIG AND RICHARD.

ABOVE: WITH TINKER AND
JOOLZ, AGED 23.

RIGHT: WITH MY GOOD FRIEND
AUNTIE NATHAN.

THE VARIOUS GUISES
OF DADDY FANTASTIC:

TOP LEFT: DADDY
FANTASTIC WITH
GROUPIES.

LEFT: DADDY FANTASTIC
AND NIMBUS THE NOODLE.

BELOW: THE BAND (LEFT
TO RIGHT): ARRON THE
BARON (BASS), ME AS
DADDY FANTASTIC AND
MY BEST FRIEND
WOBBLY BOB AS WOBBLY
BOB (ELECTRIC GUITAR).

LEFT: GOING INTO
THE BIG BROTHER
HOUSE. I JUST
REMEMBER CROWDS AND
FLASHBULBS GOING
OFF ALL OVER THE
PLACE.

BELOW: IN THE BIG
BROTHER DIARY ROOM.

TOP LEFT: LOOKING GOOD FOR THE CAMERAS.

BELOW LEFT: STRIKING A POSE. CHECK OUT THAT SMOLDERING LOOK...

BELOW RIGHT: ... AND ERR ... THEN AGAIN, MAYBE NOT!

ME, RICHARD AND ANOTHER BIG BROTHER HOUSEMATE.

TOP LEFT: ANOTHER DAY,
ANOTHER WIG!

BELOW LEFT: HAVING A CUDDLE WITH
RICHARD.

BELOW RIGHT: GETTING RE-ACQUAINTED
WITH NIKKI.

CAN'T REMEMBER WHAT I SAID BUT RICHARD CLEARLY ENJOYED IT.

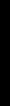

EMERGING OUT OF THE BIG BROTHER HOUSE AS WINNER. I STILL CAN'T BELIEVE IT, IT'S BEEN SUCH A MAD EXPERIENCE.

'If I ask you something will you be freaked out?' he shouted into my ear over the music.

'Probably not,' I shouted back.

'I'll give you two hundred pounds if you do something for me.'

Oh fuck, I thought, he's going to ask me to suck his knob or something. Still, better hear him out, mustn't jump to conclusions.

'Don't run away,' he went on, 'but I'd love it if you would piss in my bottle so I can have a drink.'

'Yeah, of course I'll do that,' I said, relieved. 'No worries, man.'

We went up to the toilet; I filled his bottle and we then went back down to join his mates.

'Cheers everyone,' he said, lifting the bottle and guzzled the contents down in front of everyone. I couldn't believe it.

I wouldn't have fancied it myself, but he obviously liked it because he kept coming back for more, which gave me a very useful source of extra income at a time when I needed every penny I could get together now I was an independent man about town, living an independent life.

The down side of having so many people falling in love with you and wanting to be your friend is that they tend to get all arsey when they can't have you all to themselves. I believe I always behave the same towards all the people I like. I certainly try to be friendly and genuine with everyone. But people are always getting heavy and telling me that I'm changing towards them. When I got on to *Big Brother* Lea started doing it and it pissed me off because I really liked her and I never changed in my feelings towards her, but she was sure I did, that I was acting differently. That sort of thing started to happen to me all the time in Brighton.

In fact it had been happening all my life. People always wanted to look after me, apart from the ones who wanted to beat me up and shove pencils up my nose. They would want to father me or mother me, go to bed with me or be my one and only best friend in the world. It always seemed to have to be extremes. It started when I was little, when Mum was all into the church, and the men she met there used to want to be 'father figures' to me, 'taking a paternal role'. It's nice of them, of course, better than being hated and ridiculed all the time. I'm not complaining. It's just a bit weird and difficult because I really hate hurting people's feelings but sometimes I just can't give them as much attention as they demand. Once I got to about fifteen the obsessions seemed to become more sexual, which would completely freak Mum out. You'd think all the touretting would have put them off, but it seemed to make them even more determined to help me and look after me and protect me and fuck me.

I've always been afraid of upsetting people. It's like letting goals in when I was on the football team, feeling the disappointment of the rest of the team, knowing that I'd let them down. That feeling just won't go away.

Even though I'm not gay, gay friends still sometimes become obsessed and make their whole lives revolve around me, like stalkers. Maybe if I was gay and the relationships could be consummated they wouldn't put me on this weird Perfect Pete pedestal, and then they wouldn't get so cross when I disappoint them. There have been one or two who have really freaked me out, becoming unnaturally jealous and possessive and bombarding me with letters and phone calls, accusing me of all sorts of acts of treachery and betrayal. Often they would start out being my best mates and I would try to put up with their obsessions and stay friends, but in the end it would always get out of hand. With one of them I ended up believing he could read my mind and was following me around everywhere. I became completely paranoid.

'Read your mind?' Mum said when I told her. 'Well, you know what to put in it then, don't you? Fuck off!'

Mum has good advice for virtually every situation.

Dr Mary Robertson had moved on from the hospital where I had been seeing her and had become a professor, and I didn't want to start all over again with someone new. I felt I'd had enough of doctors. There didn't seem to be any chance they were ever going to make me any better, so why go on wasting time and energy on fruitless appointments? I was who I was, and I was growing to accept that now. I didn't want to chase any more miracle cures. I decided I would just have to learn to live with my Tourette's as it mutated and developed inside me. It was all part of the 'Perfect Pete' persona, part of the performance if you like. Maybe if I was happy and relaxed it would lighten up a bit. Maybe if I stopped worrying about it and just chilled out it would stop trying to pick on me and bully me. I decided I would try ignoring it and see what happened.

Mum bumped into Mary Robertson a little while later at King's Cross tube, having gone back to doing a bit of busking due to being seriously broke once more. She was playing a 'Meditation' to the passing commuters, and became aware that a beautiful, slim, pale woman was pausing in front of her.

'That's absolutely beautiful, my dear,' the woman said, dropping a pound coin into Mum's violin case.

'It's you,' Mum said as she looked up to say thank you.

'Oh, my God,' Dr Robertson said. 'It's Pete's mum.'

It's strange how the cosmos creates those memorable little moments of coincidence out of thin air.

Mum had certain tunes that she always knew would catch the attention of passers-by, however much of a hurry they might be in, and might even elicit a few more coins from their pockets. 'Czardas' by Vittorio Monti was one that put food on our table a thousand times over the years. It's a Hungarian gypsy folk dance, which starts really slowly and then builds to a furious pace, allowing Mum to show off her skills with the bow and lifting listeners' spirits, making them smile as they trudge around the tunnels and escalators of the London Underground. I think Mum can play it faster than anyone in the world, but then I have always been a bit biased. She used to do a version of it when she was playing with the Communards and Jimmy Somerville would let her close the concert with it some nights. It must have felt great to whip a happy crowd up with a final crescendo like that. 'The Lark Ascending' by Vaughan Williams was another crowd-pleaser.

When I hear old superstars complaining that their fans only ever want to hear the same old hits from them and are never interested in anything new, I think of buskers like Mum, who have to keep playing the tunes they know will be popular over and over again unless they want to starve. In the end everyone has to use their skills to make a living in the best way they can, whether they are Sinatra or Hendrix, the Rolling Stones or Robbie Williams. Bad luck if you become famous for singing a really crap song, of course, but no one can control, or even predict, what the public wants to hear. I was to learn that big time when I came out of the *Big Brother* house and all any journalist seemed to want to know was when Nikki and I were going to 'do it'.

But I guess we should all be grateful anyone wants to hear anything from us at all.

THROUGH THE K-HOLE

Working in the cloakroom at Concorde 2, the club on the beach in Brighton, was wicked. It's not that easy to find a job in the straight world when you have as many problems as I had at the time, and when you only have an A-level in art to boast about. It's a competitive world and straight people tend to hire other straight people – why wouldn't they, we all like to be surrounded by people like ourselves, don't we? Not that I would have wanted a normal office job. It might have been fun for a bit when I was a kid on work experience, but unless there was a big creative angle to it, it wouldn't have soaked up my energies for long and I would soon have been back to howling at the moon and shouting obscenities at passers-by.

The work in the cloakroom, however, was just the right mix of soothing, repetitive movements and a stimulating background of big noise and interesting people. I found the predictable motion of taking the coats from the customers, hanging them up and giving them their tickets very comforting. At the same time I loved the buzz of different faces constantly coming and going in front of me, of the music in the background, of a big crowd out to have a good time, all giving off happy and positive vibes. The place was always full of a party spirit, lifting my spirits all the time I was there. I don't know that I would be able to do a job that didn't lift my spirits. How do people manage to get themselves out of bed day after day to do work they hate? Beats me. Hats off to them, though, because a lot of that boring stuff has to be done by someone. Then again, I guess most people would rate cloakroom attendant as being pretty low in the employment pecking order, so maybe it's just horses for courses and the perfect job is waiting out there for everyone if they are lucky enough to find it.

Above everything else, I was able to be myself when I was in that cloakroom. I didn't have to struggle to keep the demons under control because nobody cared how much I ticced or swore. Deprived of the oxygen of repression, the Tourette's didn't put so much effort into trying to torture me.

I loved Concorde 2 so much I stayed there for about two years, and turned the job into a bit of an act – cloakroom attending as a modern art form, street theatre with hangers. I could throw three coats at once at the rails and they would all catch – like James Bond tossing his hat across Miss Moneypenny's office. It was cool and people enjoyed it, I was part of their night out. I had a tip box with a message saying, 'Tip if you've got a big knob.' The guys would be with their girlfriends, so they'd have to leave something. It was great, talking to people, making them laugh. Nobody minded the Tourette's there – I was just the funny guy who looked after the coats; what difference did a bit of twitching and swearing make? The owner liked it when I called punters wankers, because often it was true.

Now everyone seemed to know me as 'Perfect Pete'. I would take my sketchbook with me and invent new cartoon characters during the quiet periods, including likenesses of the more interesting punters in the carica-tures sometimes. The club was full of wacky and won-derful people who would inspire me to think of new characters. I lost the book one time and I was broken hearted. It had about two hundred characters in it.

I met Gil at the university soon after I got to Brighton. She was gorgeous and I turned my attention to her once my broken heart felt strong enough to risk another bat-tering. She was at the university on a dance course and we both left together at the end of the first year. When I moved out of halls I moved in with her. I should have got myself organized with a flat of my own and been a bit more together about it, but I didn't know where to start. Being at Briset and Parkwood had helped a lot

with the whole independence thing, but it hadn't prepared me for organizing things like renting my own
home. One moment you're a kid having everything done
for you, the next moment you're expected to know how
to deal with landlords and local councils and God knows
what; scary enough for someone with no problems at all,
but for someone barking out swear words and twitching
every few seconds it was too much to get my head
round. Gil offered a bit of a sanctuary, a bit of a stopgap, a
breathing space.

I was totally in love with dancing and music. It was
the whole performing thing again and, like with drawing, it was one of the few activities that pushed the
Tourette's right out of my head. It was like all the energy
went into the music and movement, leaving me with no
need to tic or shout or twist about. It's a fantastic feeling
when I'm dancing, like my whole body has come alive,
like I have full control of myself, just like everyone else.

Gil and I started our own dance act, performing at
venues like the Perfumed Gardens. Gay audiences are
always very receptive to anything like that, anything a bit
different, a bit camp, a bit experimental. Part of the attrac-
tion for me was being able to dress up outrageously, just
another excuse to be an extravert and a performer, an official licence to have some fun. One of my costumes was
an angel, with my whole body painted white, my hair
brushed flat back, huge dark glasses and feathery great
wings. The Archangel Michael would have been proud!

Gil was all tricked out in silver and powder. Our performances weren't so far from the street theatre acts I'd been involved with as a tiny child, bursting out of cardboard boxes or clinging to a Vulcan's leg – just a different venue and a different audience.

Eventually I got my act together and moved into my own place, a small room in Prince's Crescent. Now I had a private little cocoon from the world. I did it up with Indian stuff, a fluffy carpet and lots of lights that flashed and moved. I always liked that sort of thing, lamps with little electrical storms inside, flickering with miniature webs of forked lightning. Stuff I could watch.

Watching any sort of repetitive movement helps to calm the Tourette's. Sometimes I sit in front of a washing machine or a tumble dryer, just staring into it, watching the washing going round and round, soothing the soul of my internal monster. It's better than telly sometimes, allowing my brain to lie fallow and dream its own dreams, devoid of outside stimulation, just churning over gently in time with the washing.

Life was good in Prince's Crescent and I was able to write lots of music on my computer with a friend called Omar, pouring all my thoughts and feelings into it without having any idea what we would do with the final product, not even really worried if there was a final product.

* * *

I first met Wobbly Bob in a café in Brighton. We had a mutual friend who worked as a cook at Concorde 2, which was how we got talking.

'Eezamanna!' was his way of greeting his mates, his catchphrase if you like; and 'easy' was what he was.

I was sitting drawing cartoons, like I do all the time, which attracted his attention because he does the same. We began improvising them together, like a sort of alternative parlour game. He would start a story, doing a few frames, and pass it to me to do a few more frames and move the story on, then I'd hand it back to him for the next bit, and so on. It was great. I loved it. It was a meeting of like minds. Wobbly was a bit older than me, in his late thirties, very tall and lanky, usually wearing a hat and sometimes an eye-patch for no apparent reason apart from the fact he liked it. He did so much great creative stuff, all of them the sort of things I was into. He loved psychedelic rock and roll and he loved *Scooby-Doo* as passionately as I loved *Beavis and Butt-head* and *Ren and Stimpy*.

Wobbly was happily trapped in 1967, the year of the 'summer of love' when Hendrix was at his peak in England, *Sgt Pepper's Lonely Hearts Club Band*, Pink Floyd's 'Piper at the Gates of Dawn' and Procul Harem's 'Whiter Shade of Pale' were released and Scott McKenzie was 'going to San Francisco'. It was a mythical golden time that happened before he was even born. It was a time when psychedelic guru Timothy Leary said, 'If you take the game of life seriously, if you take your nervous

system seriously, if you take your sense organs seriously, if you take the energy process seriously, you must
turn on, tune in and drop out.'

As well as creating his own cartoon and musical universe, Wobbly plays the electric guitar. He's a true, origi-
nal, creative rock-and-roll spirit, like so many of the
people I'd been brought up around as a child. We had so
much fun together, lost in our own world of make-
believe. It was like being back in the studio with Dave,
or inventing radio programmes with Sarah, or staying up
all night playing games and watching movies with Dale.
It was just the most fun. Magic!

By this time I had discovered ketamine, an anaesthetic
vets use to knock out animals as big as horses and ele-
phants that has awesomely powerful hallucinogenic
qualities, a bit like LSD. From the moment I heard
about what it could do I was keen to give it a go.

Vets and doctors who use it legally for operating on
animals or people get it in liquid form; those of us
who wanted to use it illegally would get it in a grainy
white powder form, which we would then cook up and
snort. Because it's an anaesthetic you can't feel much
physically when you're on it, which means there is
always a danger you'll hurt yourself without realizing,
but the trips it induces only last for about an hour. It's
quite dangerous for other reasons, too, especially if

you're drinking at the same time as using, because it can sometimes suppress breathing and heart function. It can also exaggerate any mental problems someone already has.

I knew about all these possible dangers but I didn't care because I liked the sound of it and loved the sensation once I tried it. It made me feel great and took me on the biggest trips I'd ever had. It gave me out-of-body experiences and took me to visit other planets and dimensions. It was mad, man! All my life I had been up for new experiences, always questioning what else might be going on in the universe, willing to give anything a go, wanting to see things I had never seen before. Here was a chance for all that and more.

The first time I was offered it I'd just been to a rave, where I'd had some pills. I was feeling chilled out and ready for anything. A group of us went on to an after party where I was offered a line of ketamine. I thought, OK, cool, why not? I snorted it and was immediately sucked into the wall, speeding off on a massive trip. I really liked it. It's called k-holing when you pass through to other worlds. If you only take a little bit of ketamine you just get wobbly and giggly, but I wanted to go k-holing whenever I could, just flying around, having a great time, sliding down caves and tunnels, grabbed by shadowy figures and taken to new places I could never have imagined, swimming around the universe on my own, in a bubble.

On one trip, after Gay Pride day, I was lying on a bed between a couple of friends. I turned to look at one of them and instantly got sucked into his face. Fucking hell, I thought, I'm dead. I could see my body, like a hundred miles away, and I knew I had to get back to it. As I struggled to swim back I was suddenly caught in another wave of suction which pulled me right back into my own skin, making me sit bolt upright on the bed. My mate's face was all over the walls and everyone's voices were running backwards. I thought I'd been sent back to Earth in a backwards dimension. I got up and tried to walk out of the room but I couldn't make my feet do the forward motions. I wanted to get out of there and tried to make it through the door backwards.

As I returned from another trip I was brought back in to land by a giant swan, flying through the sky above Brighton. It was holding me by the scruff of my neck in its beak and I could feel the wind on my face and everything. It was a beautiful sensation. When he finally released me from his beak I fell to earth with a cloud of feathers settling around me.

Wobbly Bob had created a brilliant cartoon series called 'Daddy Fantastic', about a rock group, and he was planning to turn it into reality, dressing himself and the other band members up in wigs and everything to look like the cartoon characters that had sprung from his imagination.

He was also writing all their music and lyrics. It was a fantastic creation. In August 2004 he asked if I would like to audition to be the lead singer, known as 'The Daddy'.

'Yeah! Definitely!' I didn't need asking twice for an opportunity like that. To be working with music and hanging out with Wobbly and the other guys were two of the best things I could imagine doing.

The audition went well and I got the job, completely taking on the persona of the cartoon, complete with a blond bob wig, big dark glasses and a cane. Whenever we played we all hid our real identities behind masks of face paint. It was a gas, an excuse to play, like being a small kid made up as Spiderman again. We did loads of gigs around Brighton. I just loved every minute of being on stage and performing and I was honoured to be a part of Wobbly's magical imaginary world. Being The Daddy suited me perfectly because when you're performing at an alternative rock gig no one cares if you shout out the odd rude word; if the timing is good it all fits together, becomes part of the persona. It all just seemed right, cosmic.

Wobbly was the lead guitarist of the band and then there was Nimbus the Noodle, the drummer, and Aaron the Baron, who played the bass in star-shaped glasses and a big afro wig. My brother Alex had a skiing hat with white dreadlocks sprouting out of it, which Noodle would wear above a scary, dramatic witchdoctor/clown-like death mask make-up.

Wobbly used to write himself great long guitar solos, going off into his own 1967 world for minutes on end, leaving me standing at the mic with nothing to do, feeling like a muppet. So I would mess about, shaving myself or whatever came to mind. One night I pulled my pants down and shaved my arse while he was playing on and on, which the audience loved. We had a bunch of zombies dancing behind us as well, one of whom was Gil. The act became a cult around Brighton and like all rock-and-rollers we dreamt of mega-recording contracts and seeing our picture on the cover of *Rolling Stone*, while vowing that we would never 'sell out' our souls to big business.

Sweet dreams are made of this.

CHAPTER TWENTY

JOOLZ

Something about the *Big Brother* programmes appealed to me. I wasn't sure why I was so fascinated, or felt so comfortable watching them, but I was. It's easy television to be with, just sitting back and letting it drift past you. In the real world you have to make an effort to participate, to play the games people inflict on you, to concentrate on what's being said even when it's boring, to try to do the right things by other people. But with television programmes you're free to just tune in and out as and when they catch your attention. No one makes any demands on you, no stress, no pressure, no expectations.

I began to wonder what it would feel like to be on the other side of the screen, to be cocooned inside that house, just as I had been cocooned so many times in my life – in the studio with Mum and Dave, in my various bedrooms, at Briset and Parkwood, in my cloakroom world at Concorde 2 and my room in Prince's Crescent. I didn't think it would be that hard for me to do.

I believed it might make me feel very happy being in there, just chilling out with the other people, under the protective eye of Big Brother.

Just before they started casting for *Big Brother 5*, in 2003, I had a dream that I was in the house and, like so many of my dreams, it felt completely real. There was just one other girl there, a blonde, who I didn't recognize. I liked the feeling of the cameras being there, watching over me, guarding me and observing me performing at the same time. The same dream happened several times and I thought, Fuck; maybe I should audition to go into the house. Maybe I should make the dream a reality. Maybe the dreams are a sign.

The more I thought about it the more I realized that being inside the *Big Brother* house would be a nice feeling. I would be safe and I wouldn't have to worry about anything, protected by the cameras and by Big Brother. I might even win some prize money – how cool would that be?

I applied and set off for the auditions in high spirits and a pink bowler hat. All through the day I held the Tourette's in as much as I could, even though it hurt, not wanting to alarm the production team and make them think I wouldn't make suitable family viewing. The whole process went really well. I was sufficiently absorbed in what was going on for the pain of holding in the tics and twitches to be bearable. Mum had moved on from the Catholic Church and become a Buddhist by then, and she'd taught me how to do chanting if you want to get something to happen, to push your life in a positive direction. So I'd been doing a bit of that and it seemed to have worked.

'Nam Myoho Renge Kyo.'

I got more and more confident that I was going to get into the house as the day wore on and I kept being put through to the next round, to the next test, the next task. But then they set up some competitive games which involved being confrontational, and I immediately started to flounder. I just couldn't do it. I've never been any good at arguing. I don't know how people do it. I used to try to stick up for myself at school when I was little and I would always end up getting beaten up for my trouble, which didn't encourage me to try again. It was hard enough to control the Tourette's as it was; it was impossible to keep a handle on it under the stress of confrontation.

I felt so sad when I realized I wasn't going to get through to the end. I'd grown so confident with each little triumph through the day that to be knocked back at the last fence was hard. I'd used up every ounce of energy trying to keep all the Tourette's inside and to control every movement for so many hours. Exhausted, I slept for about two days straight once I got home.

Although it was disappointing at the time, my failure to be accepted turned out to be for the best. The people in *Big Brother 5* were very different to the ones I would later be with. It was a much more aggressive and competitive atmosphere and I don't think I would have survived long with them because I hadn't yet found the courage to completely be myself in front of other people. If I had always been trying to cover up the Tourette's and disguise who I really was, eventually I would have exploded and given myself away. I don't think anyone would have voted for me if I had been pretending to be someone different. The public are good at sniffing out phoneys and charlatans. My time hadn't come and I had to accept that. It was hard but I'd overcome bigger disappointments and setbacks in my life. I put it down to an interesting experience and went back to enjoying my life in Brighton.

After only a few months I had to leave the place in Prince's Crescent because the landlord needed it back for some reason. I wasn't sure where to go next and asked around everyone I knew. A mate suggested I called another friend of his, a guy called Joolz.

'He's got a place,' he said. 'I know there are rooms there.'

I rang the number he gave me.

'Hi,' I said, touretting away nervously. 'I'm Perfect Pete, I hear you've got a room.'

'Yeah, all right,' the voice at the other end said, apparently unbothered by all my coughing, throat clearing and swearing as I tried to get the words out. 'Come and have a look.'

I went to the address he gave me in Shaftesbury Place and found a tall, traditional-style house backing on to the London Road railway station. Inside it had a staircase running up the centre and rooms off to either side. I could tell the moment I walked through the door that this was my kind of place, and Joolz was a completely cool man. He had painted his own room blood red and it was filled with pentangles, demonic symbols and numerology stuff. The whole house was a real tip, more like a squat than a home, and I loved it. It didn't worry me that there was smashed furniture everywhere, rubbish and newspapers piled high and windows all blacked out with sheets, I just knew this was a place where I would have a lot of fun and that this was a man I wanted to get to know better. It had really good vibes, and Joolz and I got on instantly, like we had known each other for the whole of eternity. I loved it and agreed to move in for fifty quid a week.

Joolz was a musician, the lead guitarist with a group called Aped Bi Sapien, which was signed to the Undergroove label and played regularly at venues like Concorde 2 and the Free Butt pub. People who knew about the music business were saying they were about to be really big and they were booked to do a national tour as a support band. Joolz had learnt the guitar and cello at school and college in Haywards Heath, a commuter town a few stops inland on the train. He was really buzzing with the excitement of it all, and recruiting musicians to work with him, so I persuaded him to ring Mum and see if she could play for him. It never happened but it would have been great if it had. They would have been brilliant together.

He looked amazing, with wild black hair, piercings and tattoos everywhere, the incredible illustrated man, really beautiful looking, a human work of art. The tattoos on his back rose from a point at the base of his spine, spreading out up to his shoulders in an intricate atomic explosion. His limbs were living works of art, like the graffiti on a New York subway. He was about the same age as me, and crazy too, mental, loads of fun, really naughty. He didn't give a fuck what people thought, just didn't care. He was up for anything and as a result everybody loved him. I moved in and for nearly a year we had a brilliant time. He earned a bit of money doing telesales just to keep himself afloat while he waited for the music to pay off.

We used to jam around the house all the time, both of us absorbed in our music. It was a madhouse and there was so much going on we couldn't really find any time to clean up after ourselves. That's an excuse; we actually couldn't be bothered, didn't want to bring ourselves down with housework. The muck and grime built up cheerfully around us, everything dark and dingy, piles of rubbish expanding everywhere, but we didn't care, we had other things on our minds, other vistas to dream about. This was our own private universe and to us it was beautiful.

No one ever came asking for any rent. One day I came downstairs and bumped into a bloke mending a pipe or something, who told me he was the landlord. I asked if he wanted some rent and gave him four hundred quid but we never saw the guy again. Must just have been a plumber.

After a while my mate Tinker moved in with us too, and Dice Face, so called because of all the dice piercings in his face – obviously! I'd met Tinker about the same time I met Wobbly Bob. He worked as a masseur and from the moment we met we seemed to link up cosmically, both of us always knowing where the other one was and how we were feeling at any given moment of the day.

'Are you a witch?' was the first thing he asked me when we met.

'Nah,' I replied with a cheerful tourettey grimace. 'I'm a what.'

'I can't believe you just said that,' he laughed happily. 'I'm a what too.'

From that moment the spiritual link was forged. He was very beautiful, with long hair, and was completely mad about sex. One night there was a dead deer lying in the field where we were partying and we stood staring at it for a while, pondering the meaning of life and death and the whole cosmic thing.

'Shall we fuck it?' Tinker wondered out loud.

Although I laughed so much I cried, I was never completely sure that he was joking.

'We're going to meet a nice dark-haired dancing girl called Cherry,' we told each other one day, as we sat around the house talking about whatever came into our heads. We had already discovered that we both loved cherries more than any other fruit, so it seemed like an obvious progression. A few days later we met a dancer called Cherry at a party after a field rave. It was like Mum and her positive visualization technique; we pictured her and then we found her – really strange and really good to be so in tune with the universe, to be having our wishes fulfilled by some invisible force.

Cherry was an exotic dancer and immediately became a good friend too, coming round the house a lot to hang out. I began to feel myself being drawn to her, although I knew she had a boyfriend and was out of bounds.

We had so many new friends: Auntie Nathan, Smiley-Steve, Craig and Richard, Monique – life was just one big buzz, so much love and so much laughing. I suppose in the great cosmic balancing act there were bound to be tears eventually.

FETISH PARTIES

I've always thought that you should try everything life has to offer at least once, so when I heard about the fetish scene I thought I would like to see what it was all about. It sounded interesting, all that dressing up and camping about, another sort of performance art really, street theatre behind closed doors, party games for grown-ups. There was a club in London called the Torture Garden, claiming to 'celebrate sexuality and fantasy'. I liked the sound of that, especially when I heard they played hard techno music, which always made me feel totally happy and at one with the cosmos. I went up to town with a couple of girlfriends who knew all about it to try it out. I knew you had to dress up if you wanted to get in, so I'd got myself a black fetish shirt, but I was just wearing some casual blue tie-pants on my bottom half.

'You're not getting in here with those on,' the door people told me, staring disdainfully at my legs.

When I looked around at who was getting in I could see that the dress code was a bit stricter than I'd realized. Kinky and perverse was what it was all about, extreme, loads of black leather, rubber, PVC, S&M, uniforms, body art, straps, fishnets, chains and full drag, but definitely no blue tie-pants.

'I haven't got anything else with me,' I pleaded, hoping they would make an exception, as it was my first time.

'You can't come in then.' Their faces had that stony 'can't hear you, can't see you, you don't exist' look that bouncers get when you're starting to annoy them, like a bluebottle round a cow's arse. I could tell there was no chance of getting round them with charm or even blatant begging.

'How do I get in then?' I asked.

'Either borrow something off someone else or take 'em off.'

I couldn't think of anything I could borrow off anyone, so I thought, OK, fuck it, and I took my pants off, immediately walking through the door with their blessing and my knob hanging out. No one else seemed bothered, quite the opposite. I instantly knew it had been worth the hassle; the music was mental, the outfits brilliant. There were all different ages, sexes, orientations, colours, sizes and types gyrating around us, a really great scene, a real laugh. There were dungeons and playrooms, people strung up in harnesses, fashion shows and live sex shows on stage, fire eaters and DJs. I wandered around the whole carnival with my mouth hanging open – wow!

I liked it so much I went again, with a better outfit this time; a short black dress, lots of straps, and black boots. No trouble from the doormen this time. I was now officially one of them.

The club came to Brighton, like the universe was arranging things just for my convenience, so I started going there too. I was there for the music as much as anything else, wicked, hard techno, and I left everyone else to get on with their naughty bits, being pierced on stage or spanked in harnesses. It all created a brilliant surreal atmosphere and I danced like a man possessed to the thump of the base.

Joolz enjoyed the scene as much as I did. I loved him so much. We were both so confident of our friendship we could cross any boundaries together and it was never anything other than a laugh. We used to have sword fights with our knobs, battling for supremacy. He had a massive one too and we were so close we could do that sort of thing without it having any sexual connotation, like kid brothers messing around together at bath time.

People were whispering about a secret party planned in a hidden-away mansion in Kent. I was used to listening to these sorts of rumours; that was how I got to hear about illegal field raves and other events – it was how you found out what was on at short notice. It sounded so decadent, so anarchic, so much like some novelist's fantasy. I let it be known I was interested. All my friends from the techno scene said they wanted to come too because they'd heard about the power of the music the clubs played on the fetish scene. Cherry came too, looking totally gorgeous, as we all got strapped up in the gear. On the first visit I wore a tutu, a pair of red wings and a chain around my neck.

When we got there it was even more extreme than anything I'd been to at the clubs, being a private party with nobody in danger of losing any licence or being raided by the police. There were people being hung up from the ceiling on hooks, and tug of war games going on with the ropes tied to rings pierced into the contestants' backs. Upstairs a man was hanging from the ceiling being lashed with a cat-o'-nine-tails, the walls all around him covered with projections of fetish porno films. It was great, a fabulous, sexy nightmare of a scene, a reason to dress up and dance and meet extraordinary people, new people, weird people. I went back and back.

I bumped into Lizzie-Anne again at a fetish night, the transsexual who had looked after me as a child. It seemed strange to see her now I was a grown-up, but the even stranger thing was that we discovered she'd looked after Tinker when he was a kid too. Cosmic coincidence or what? Everybody's favourite tranny nanny. Tinker and I truly were spiritual brothers, living parallel lives. Fucking mental!

The mansion parties became a regular feature of our night lives and one night I found myself locked into some stocks in a ground-floor room, being horse-whipped across the back by Joolz while I tripped my nut off on acid.

I really liked the attention and the next time Tinker took over the whipping, hitting much harder, taking it much more seriously. There were a few 'inspectors' standing around making sure he was doing it right at the same time as enjoying the show. I was facing a window out over the grounds of the house and the rest of my friends were gathered outside to watch the live show. I was loving it. I found I went past the pain barrier and then didn't feel the lashes any more, no matter how hard Tinker whipped. Once the pain had gone the blows just brought on a high, a rush of endorphins to the brain, releasing tensions, clearing pathways to new places. I liked to see how far I could push it before I had to ask them to stop. It was a wicked feeling and I went back time and again for more, giving everyone a go at beating me, a whole room full of people in the end – welcome to Pete's whipping party!

It was one great big brilliant party with me at its swirling centre. I remembered Freddy Krueger from the *Nightmare on Elm Street* movies, how he enjoyed being beaten as a boy, confusing pain and pleasure – now I was living in the middle of 'nightmare on Pete Street'.

'Wow! Yeah! Whip me again! Hit me, hit me! I'm loving it.'

I would end up covered in vivid red stripes but really buzzing and floating in my head.

A big fat lady came up during one of the whippings.

'Ooh, I like you,' she purred, pursing her lips and wiggling an electric prod around my balls and arse. 'Wow!' Quite liked that sensation too, the carnival just rolled on and on.

I made another new friend at a mansion party, Gareth, who was working as a gardener. He came back to my place afterwards and we found we liked a lot of the same techno stuff. Later he got together with a girl called Ashley, a hippy working in a clothes shop, and I had a vision that they were going to have a baby boy together. The vision came true and Ashley discovered she had conceived on the same night I'd seen it predicted. They had a baby boy called Jack and asked me to be his godfather – how wicked is that? Perfect Pete the Godfather. Move over Marlon Brando.

But I'm getting ahead of myself. There were dark and terrible times to come for all of us before young Jack would make his appearance in the world.

THE NIGHT OF THE 23RD

Joolz had this thing about the number twenty-three. He even had it tattooed on his chest in big Latin numerals, which looked really intense and really beautiful. Lots of people have the same feeling about the number, believing it has magical powers. Apparently it occurs all the time in the Bible in the book of Genesis, all to do with prosperity and wealth and also to do with death. I never got too much into it myself, but I was willing to go along for the ride. Everyone is entitled to their own set of beliefs, man.

On 23 October 2004, Joolz wanted to celebrate the date and we were partying the night away after a good day on the beach, watching the waves and the sky and the people passing by as we lay on the pebbles, listening to the distinctive squawk of the gulls. It had been a pleasant autumn day at the seaside and we walked back home to Shaftesbury Place afterwards as it grew dark, already tripping out. The fun went on in the house until the early hours of Sunday morning, everyone happy and some of them dropping off to sleep, dreaming, flying, whatever. We were all trashed.

The exact order of events after that is confused in my head now, but at some stage Joolz, Cherry and I decided to play a game we'd made up. We then found ourselves back outside the house in the empty, silent night street, creeping around on all fours, messing about in the mud and puddles being created by a sudden rainstorm. None of us really knew what was happening, nor cared, we were just enjoying being alive and partying in our own private world. I was high as a kite on magic mushrooms and tripping my nuts off, feeling perfect, all my senses heightened, a superman, enjoying all the dazzling colours swirling round inside my head, wearing nothing but my boxer shorts, not feeling the cold or the wet, not feeling anything. I was watching Joolz. He had on boxer shorts too and a T-shirt covering most of his tattoos.

Creeping, crawling, laughing, talking nonsense, we found ourselves on the deserted station platform next door. Joolz crept on over the bridge and dropped down on to the lines, crunching on the shingle, while Cherry and I laughed and laughed. Everything seemed so funny.

'You look like Gollum,' I called out to him.

We were his audience and he was playing up to us, giving a crouched, animated, comical performance. He touched one of the dead rails, pretending it was live and that the electric current had stung him. He was hamming it up and we were laughing more and more uncontrollably. At the back of my mind I knew railway lines had the power to kill, but I assumed Joolz knew what he was doing. Maybe I assumed they turned the current off at night. Maybe I just didn't take the time to think about it at all. It was a black comedy, a joke, nothing to think deeply about. It was funny and I was happy and high and not thinking straight about anything really.

Joolz crept further on to the tracks as he continued his performance, then he suddenly slumped on to the rails and I saw a spark fly off him. I still thought he was messing around and I was still laughing. It looked like he was still jiggling about laughing too, pretending to be electrocuted. I can't remember which of us stopped laughing first. I think it was Cherry.

'Fuck, Joolz!' she screamed.

Even in my numb state I could tell something had changed in our game, that something had gone terribly wrong. She wasn't being funny. It wasn't a joke any more. Something serious was happening. I tried to force my brain to focus clearly on what was going on, tried to work it out logically, but it wasn't making sense, I couldn't do it. I couldn't bring myself fully back to reality yet. I was too far away.

We both managed to run down on to the track as fast as we could, both shouting, trying to work out what to do, panicking and struggling not to. Without thinking we each grabbed one of his legs to pull him off. There was an enormous explosion as the current hit us and we were thrown back as if we'd been hit by a thousand dump trucks. It was like an earthquake inside my whole body.

We didn't know what to do. We were just two stoned, lost kids messing about in our underwear and this was serious, this was life and death, not a game at all. Fucking hell! We ran screaming from the station, back to the house, kicking the door in, shouting for Tinker who was upstairs, not knowing what else to do. We needed help, guidance, advice, instructions, but we didn't know who to turn to for any of it. It was like we were trapped in some other dimension, trying to make urgent contact with the real world and not able to get through.

'Joolz is dead! Joolz is dead!' I screamed, unable to believe that the words I could hear coming out of my mouth could actually be true.

Maybe it was just a bad trip, maybe we would come down in a minute and everything would start to make sense again, going back to normal.

Whether it was a trip or not, I knew my best friend was still frazzling on the line and we had to get him off, but there wasn't anything we could do. We were helpless. I was freaking out, no idea how much time was passing, no idea how to get help. Tinker came running out of the house and back out to the station with me, trying to make sense of my terrified jabberings. We could see Joolz from the platform, still juddering on the line, sparks and smoke coming off his face. I'd completely lost it, like my whole life had collapsed on top of me, like I was watching the scene from afar, detached and unable to reach it but aware that it was real. We slumped helplessly down on to the platform, not knowing what to do, just waiting for someone else to come to save us.

A neighbour living in the real world in a nearby house must have heard our shouts and called an ambulance. It took half an hour to come, and the smell of burning was terrible – we had to leave Joolz for all that time, completely helpless and useless.

The police arrived with the ambulance and the world of sober, capable adults took over. They all knew what to do to remove him. They took charge. They covered him, restored his dignity, lifted him gently into the ambulance, kind hands and hearts doing their best to clear up the terrible mess we had created. It was the last time I would see him apart from in my dreams and visions. We would only ever meet in other dimensions now.

Once they had taken care of Joolz they told Cherry and me officially that he was dead and took us to hospital to treat us for shock. I had really bad chest pains and Cherry kept jerking in the aftermath of the electricity; both of us were traumatized. I felt more closely bonded with Cherry after that night than I had ever felt before. We'd travelled from heaven to hell in the space of a few seconds and now we had landed back in the straight world where we'd started our journey; it didn't seem possible that so much had happened in such a short time, that so many endless minutes of fear and agony could have been contained in just half an hour.

Back in the real world I couldn't get my head round what had happened, couldn't stop shaking and crying. Anyone who believed in the magic that is supposed to surround the number twenty-three would have been convinced they had seen yet another demonstration of its power. I had no idea what to believe in because everything had become a senseless chaos.

CHAPTER TWENTY-THREE

HEAVEN AND HELL

In a completely different dimension of my life, Mum had found a house to move to in Honfleur, in France. She wanted to start a new life for herself away from all the nastiness of South London. It was a good move for Alex too because he's really bright and good academically, so he would have been in danger of being picked on and bullied in the streets around Eltham just like I'd been, only for different reasons. I was missing them, but Normandy isn't so far and I was a grown-up now with a life of my own. I hardly ever went back to Eltham anyway, for fear of being attacked, so I would probably see more of them once they'd moved to France.

The Well Hall Road was still a terrible place to live, possibly even worse than when we moved there, either crammed with traffic jams or a race track for speeding joy riders, depending on the time of day or night. When a woman with a baby in a pushchair was killed by a car almost outside the house, her face gruesomely disfigured,

Mum felt she'd finally had enough. There was no reason to stay there any longer if she had an option. Thanks to a mortgage from a kindly bank manager she'd been able to buy the house off the council, so now she sold it and used the money as a deposit on a new home in Honfleur.

She'd waited till she thought I was going to be able to cope on my own, till I seemed to have become a grown-up. She took Alex with her, to put him into a French school. He wouldn't have any trouble adjusting to a new country. He could pick up a language in no time. He'd turned into such a cool guy, really wicked!

When everything went wrong with Joolz I didn't feel like such a grown-up any more. I really needed my mum again. I needed her to sort me out, tell me what to do next, give me a bit of a scolding and tidy everything up. My brain had gone bananas from the shock and the Tourette's had taken over big-time, sending my tics and twitches into orbit. Even the simplest task seemed like climbing a mountain. I phoned her up and she came back to help me sort out the house, and to be there while I cried.

There was an eviction order on us and we had to get out of the house in Shaftesbury Place, so Mum went to the council and explained to them that I was about to be made homeless. They took pity and sorted me out with a flat where someone was employed to pop in now and then to check I was all right, a bit like mildly sheltered accommodation. It was like stepping back towards Briset and Parkwood, giving me a light crutch to lean on as I tried to reorientate myself and regain my balance.

I'd been meaning to audition for the next *Big Brother*, but there was no way my head was together enough for that now. I could barely make myself understood at all through all the contortions and swear words; I could hardly expect to be welcomed with open arms by a television programme. I would never have passed the psychiatric tests anyway. I needed time to sort myself out, to find some equilibrium and a platform to start rebuilding from.

I'd already fallen in love with Cherry, and now I felt bonded even more tightly to her by the experience of that night together, the worst night of either of our lives. But she still had a boyfriend, so I couldn't do anything about it. I would never break up someone else's relationship, but I wanted to be with her all the time. My head was so messed up it was hard to work out what was going on.

Having been through such a real ordeal, experienced real pain and suffering close up, I no longer wanted to have anything to do with the fetish parties. It would have been grotesque to play at such things after what had happened to Joolz, disrespectful to his memory. It felt like it was time to grow up a bit, to start acting like an adult maybe, if I could just work out how it was done. But that didn't mean I didn't still want to let my hair down and dance and have fun as the months drifted past and life kept rolling on. I needed to be able to forget all the bad stuff for a little time at least. In fact I needed the music and dancing more than ever, like an escape valve on a pressure cooker that's set to explode.

On New Year's Eve, as our lives trudged towards 2005, I heard about an illegal psychedelic trance rave to be held in Lewes Fire Station. I was looking forward to it. All my friends were going to be there. The moment I walked in I could see it was going to be really good; great music, great people, but I could feel I wasn't getting into the mood properly.

A friend suggested we should drop some acid to see the New Year in, which seemed like a good idea. I needed to put some bright colours into my head. I took one drop, but it didn't seem to be working, so I took another, and then another. Three drops gone but I still didn't seem to be going anywhere. I snorted some proffered ketamine as well to try to get things kick-started. For a split second there was nothing and then all three of the drops of acid cut in at the same time as I k-holed through the wall, totally tripping out as I started to dance to the beat.

It was an incredible feeling. I was tripping and k-holing simultaneously. I was on the way up, feeling optimistic. Then the brakes screamed on and my ascent crashed to a halt, cruelly interrupted by the thought of Joolz's death, a really bad feeling, dragging part of me back down to earth. I suddenly felt like shit. I had to get out of the party, had to try to clear my head and work out what I wanted to do. I stumbled outside into the cold night air, my trip disintegrating around my feet. I was missing Joolz so much it was like a physical pain.

There were other things in my head bothering me too, like my unrequited feelings for Cherry and my worries about Mum and her money problems. Everything that worried or upset me was swelling up like a tidal wave, threatening to overwhelm me as I sat with my head in my hands, unable to cope with the prospect of another night of depression. I was feeling more upset than I could ever remember being. I'd come to the party to enjoy myself and forget all the bad stuff and now I was sinking lower than ever before. I couldn't see how this cycle of despair could ever end. Was I doomed to be this wretchedly miserable for the rest of my life?

Hang on a minute, I thought to myself. What would Joolz think about this? I know exactly what he would be thinking; he'd be wanting me to enjoy myself. He always wanted people to enjoy themselves; he loved fucking great parties. So that's what I have to do. I have to have a fucking wicked New Year's Eve. For Joolz.

I knew it was up to me not to have a shit time. I just needed to jump-start my mood change. I stood up, breathed deeply, felt my spirits rising already and danced back into the party, recharged and ready for anything. The mood change had worked and I started back on the ascent, letting the music take a hold and direct my body around the dance floor. Everyone was applauding me as I sped back up to the beat of the base, my tourettey dance movements taking over and throwing my limbs about, mad, happy, having a great time, spinning round the room in a circle. The Perfect Pete dance. I was partying again, back at the centre of everything. Life was going to go on after all.

'Yeah Pete! Yeah Pete!' The whole room was cheering and clapping me, pushing me further up.

I rose higher and higher, dancing faster and faster, feeling myself floating away from the real world, aware that everyone was joining in with me, all around me. It felt like I'd cracked the whole meaning of life. I found myself inside a spiral and I knew that, piece-by-piece, I had managed to find the code to everything. This was the code I needed to get to heaven, to understand all the answers to all the questions I had ever asked. Each of my tourettey movements was part of the code too, just as long as I kept up the momentum. It was a fabulous feeling. I started chanting, spouting a great long speech as the trance music kept thumping through me, going faster and faster. Everyone was clapping me because it was my time, my moment. They were clapping me because I was pushing out all the shit in my head; the sight of Joolz dying, the fact that I didn't have a proper girlfriend, that Mum was skint and didn't have a decent man. I was pushing it all away to get to a better place. It was all coming together. Everything was spinning, faster and faster and faster. It built and built with the music and the movement and the clapping and then there was a sensation like a spacecraft taking off, a gunning of engines, a huge roaring expulsion of air mixing with the throbbing of the beat and the spinning of the room. I was shot upwards and everyone in the room came with me. We were on our way to somewhere else, to another dimension, no longer in a provincial fire station.

Suddenly I found myself inside the massive spiral and I could see that it was made up of every single person I had ever met in my whole life. Each step of the spiral as I made my way up was another Tourette's twitch. Everything pulsated with the most intense, shimmering colours I had ever experienced and everyone I met looked perfect and beautiful, glowing with health and happiness and goodness. I realized I was going to heaven and that everyone was happy to see me there, all of them laughing. It was like everyone in heaven had gathered to throw me a surprise party.

'You bastards!' I laughed as each of them came forward to shake me by the hand and hug me.

In the few seconds I spent with each of them we went through everything that had ever happened between us, our whole lives flashing before our eyes like drowning

men. I was falling deeply in love with each of them, over
and over again, one after another. We connected, locked
eyes and became one another, merging together. I was
making peace with everyone, clicking and falling in love.
Jim Carrey and Billy Idol were there, guest stars appearing
in this celebration of the story of my life. It was so much
fun, the greatest party ever, going on and on for hours.
There were tweety-birds flying all round my head, like a
Disney cartoon, and ripe cherries everywhere I looked.

At the top of the spiral were my family: Mum, Dad
and Alex, Nan and Grandad, aunts and uncles, and my
close circle of friends like Tinker and Cherry. Everything
any of us wanted to do or have was given to us, so there
I was making love with Cherry in heaven – wow!
Everything was perfect.

There's one person missing, I thought. Someone's not
here. Who is it? I could feel a presence and I just went
mental.

'Joolz! Fucking hell!'

He stood in front of me, his arms wide open in welcome, looking really happy. I had never been so excited
to see anyone in my entire life. It was the best feeling ever
because I had missed him so much. We grabbed each
other and clung on tight, floating and dancing and com-
municating. We started to melt into each other, spinning
and spinning, faster and faster.

I could hear the beginning of a tune that I'd recorded, 'Mockingbird', dig-a-dee, dig-a-dee, dig-a-dee. I was

whistling and beat boxing. I'd made a CD of the song a little while before, including a sampled Jim Carrey line from his movie *Dumb and Dumber*. The two main characters, Carrey and Jeff Daniels, are in their car, which is fluffy like a dog.

'Wish we had a radio,' Daniels says.

'Who needs a radio,' Carrey mugs and starts singing, 'Mockingbird!'

The tune now seemed to contain everything about my life. Joolz was playing along to it with his guitar, Billy Idol was singing it and all my friends were going mad, joining in like my song was the greatest anthem ever. All the silly noises that I make, like the meowing and the beat boxing and the popping, all became part of the music, as well as every other beautiful sound I had ever liked. Heaven had remixed a trance version of my 'Mockingbird' – wow! How cool was that? As we spun on up to the top of the spiral I heard a new voice over all the others.

'There really is such a place as heaven,' it boomed.

I knew it was God's voice. It had to be, he was the only one not yet at the party. I'd reached the top of the spiral, exploding through to a crescendo of the 'Mockingbird' soundtrack – my tune, filling heaven like the show-stopping finale of the greatest musical ever. Everyone was dancing around, millions of souls all together in the dazzling, spiralling colours, blues, pinks, silvers, everyone loving one another. I could see everyone for who they really were, their true spirits, and they were all beautiful. Everything had clicked into place and there was nothing more to worry about.

I met myself and made peace with all my demons and insecurities. I looked down at my body and it had become beautiful, all muscular and perfect, no longer its puny old shape. I was sure at that moment that I must have died and gone to heaven and it was the most wonderful feeling in the world. It felt like I'd been up there for eternity, and then I heard my friends all shouting warnings.

'Noooo, Pete!'

They all reached down and tried to grab my arms to stop me falling, but I was on my way down, back to my body, and there was nothing they could do to save me.

When I woke up in a bed in Brighton General Hospital, surrounded by policemen, I was convinced I was in hell. I had no memory of how I'd got there. The last thing I remembered was the slide down from heaven. What the fuck had happened? I couldn't understand why I'd been sent back down. What had I done wrong? Why was I being punished? My whole personality seemed to have disappeared, no emotions left. I must have been sent to hell for something I'd done wrong in the past, what other explanation could there be?

Tinker came to the hospital to get me, taking me outside into the cold winter air blowing up from the sea, and once I got home I still had no life left in me. Everything seemed grey and nasty. I couldn't dance or draw or be happy, it was like all the life had been drained out of me. I'd forgotten how to be Perfect Pete or The Daddy or any of the other characters that had been so much part of who I was. I was just flat, like I'd died.

I went to another party as soon as I could and tried to dance but my movements were all jagged and back-to-front, I couldn't recapture whatever it was I'd been doing before, couldn't crack the code. I couldn't connect to any of my friends. I was all at sea, cut off and in a weird head state, not able to understand what they were saying, like there was a barrier between us. Sometimes I didn't even know who they were. I thought they were sent from hell to pretend they didn't know anything about heaven, didn't know any of the code, in order to distract me from trying to get back.

People told me that I'd been found running round the fire station car park, screaming and shouting, and the police had been called because no one could control me. Once the police had realized I was harmless the only thing they could think to do was take me to the hospital. I didn't remember any of that. That was the limbo between heaven and hell and it had been wiped from my memory.

Convinced as the days went by that I was now dwelling in hell, trapped like the walking dead, a bit like Freddy Krueger, I cut my hair into weird pigtails with different coloured ribbons in it. I'd gone from being 'Perfect Pete' to 'Pigtail Pete'. I was a different person. I kept having tantalizing flashbacks of the first part of the code that led up to heaven, as if my friends up there were trying to help me remember, trying to get me back. Sometimes I would get a few feet up the spiral again but then I would lose the next bit of the code and come sliding back down.

By that time I was hooked on ketamine psychologically, although not physically. I constantly wanted to be k-holing to other dimensions, desperate to get back to heaven. It was all I thought about. How to find the code again to get back. It felt like it was my fault everyone had been dragged back down because I couldn't remember the code. I developed a new obsession where I had to follow things down the right-hand side because that would be the only way to find the way back to heaven.

I had totally lost it.

CRACKING THE CODE

At the inquest into Joolz's death a lot of people talked about what a close-knit group of friends we were.

'It was a measure of the group's close friendship that they tried to rescue Joolz,' a British Transport policeman said. 'They were a very, very close-knit group of friends. I would assess that he was electrocuted and lost consciousness immediately.'

Joolz's dad said, 'Joolz was a big bundle of fun, an extremely supportive and loving son, highly intelligent, intuitive, understanding and inquisitive.' No matter what happens to them in life, everyone was someone's baby once.

The coroner recorded a verdict of accidental death. 'I find myself very moved,' she said, 'by this inquest and by the close friendship and love that existed between all involved.'

It seems strange to think of that terrible dark, surreal nightmare being discussed in the cold, sober light of day by kind, serious-minded people, all of them trying to understand how such a thing could have happened on a deserted railway track at a time of night when most good people were asleep in their beds. Sometimes I wondered if it had really happened at all, or whether it was just another trip, like the ride with the giant white swan. Then reality would hit me and I would remember that it was real and I would feel sick all over again. When you are twenty-three you don't expect people around you to die. It's not the way things are supposed to be and it makes you think about things you might not otherwise think about for years. Young people die in other places, as strangers on the front pages of newspapers, but not friends, not in front of your eyes. People you know should be exempt from such finality. There should be time to tell them all the things you want to tell, time to make sure they know how much you love them. Until the moment when the unthinkable happens, it feels like they are immortal because you never have thought for a moment about their mortality.

My main preoccupation still was how to get back up to heaven, and I worked constantly at the puzzle. How to crack the code again, that was my obsession. But the answer wouldn't come to me. It was always just out of reach, taunting me with my own inability to stretch out and grasp it. I was determined to keep living my life, to keep trying to solve it. Sometimes, when I snorted ketamine, I would be able to retrieve a small part of the code from my memory, and my hopes would be raised. But it was never enough to get back up the spiral. I felt there was a trap door in my head that I needed to get access to, but I couldn't find it however hard I searched. I began to believe I would be trapped in hell forever. I felt suicidal. Tinker told me he'd had a similar experience. He understood exactly what I was talking about.

As my drawing powers came back a little I did a cartoon of myself, dreaming of the spiral to heaven and holding a noose in my hand, considering the possibility of ending it all if I couldn't find the solution.

'Hello there,' I wrote beside the bedraggled figure. 'I'm Perfect Pete. I'm not really happy at the moment. Check it out.'

I was having a go at getting a normal life together. I'd been down to the job centre and talked to the disability team to see what I might be able to do. I didn't have much of a history to give them. There had been the job at Concorde 2, and then there had been the dancing at the Perfumed Gardens and some street theatre. I'd done some design work for club nights called White Rhino, making fliers for them. All these things showed I was willing to work, but they didn't exactly make it obvious what direction I should be looking in. Not your standard CV material exactly. It had always been hard getting people to pay me for doing things, and I was not good at asking for money, especially when it was stuff that I enjoyed doing anyway.

I'd done a bit of modelling in the past for some mates running fetish nights as well, for pictures they could use on their fliers. It was a good laugh, pictures all over Brighton of me chained to beds and stuff, which someone later sold to a tabloid, pretending they were for real rather than posed. Another friend took pictures of me in a forest for her art portfolio, and those pictures ended up being sold to newspapers too.

Mum was getting quite frustrated with me. I guess she was worried she was going to have to be sorting me out for the rest of her life when she actually wanted to get on with her new life in France. I felt bad about being a burden again. I really did want to get my act together but the Tourette's made everything doubly hard.

The following summer I decided to go to a techno party in a field, hoping to lose myself like I always used to when dancing to the music. I dropped some acid in the car on the way over with a friend. It was really strong and I started to feel my mood improving almost immediately. We had to stop to pick up some pieces of a sound system and I got out of the car to help. Looking down at the floor I noticed it looked extraordinary. It didn't feel like a normal acid trip at all. I saw loads of faces looking up at me but they weren't happy faces, they were like

dead souls, a sea of them staring mournfully up at me.
I hadn't done acid for a long time but this wasn't how I
remembered it. I remembered it as being all beautiful
and colourful. I began to feel scared.

We got back into the car and drove to a garage so my
friend could buy petrol. I was feeling strange. I tried getting out for some air but it didn't help. I climbed back
into the safety of the car. I heard the engine roar back
into life and as we pulled forward a vast gate to hell
appeared in front of us. We drove straight at it and I
started screaming, realizing I was now right at the bottom of the spiral. I had been following right-hand turns
all this time and it had been the wrong way, taking me
down instead of up. I was filled with a terrible dread that
I had run out of time and would never be able to get
back up now.

'Pete, calm down, calm down,' my friend shouted.
'You'll be all right.'

I knew I had to trust him, even though he was turning into an evil-looking being in front of my eyes.

I had to remember the code quickly or I was going to
be going straight to hell. I concentrated as hard as I
could, my eyes closed, thinking, thinking, thinking, trying to force the spiral to take me up away from the gate.
All the way to the party I kept concentrating with my
eyes closed, trying desperately to work it out. We arrived
at the party but I still hadn't got it, still didn't dare to
open my eyes as I got out of the car, thinking all the

time. I was off my nut, rolling around on the ground, convinced I was in a bush and being forced to have sex with a stinking old hag who had maggots falling out of her fanny. Once I had been Perfect Pete and I could make love to beautiful girls, but now I was Pigtail Pete, living in hell and having to have sex with hags.

Then I saw it. I could see the path.

'I've found it, I've found it,' I shouted, jumping to my feet, eyes still tightly shut, running down the field towards the code that I could see ahead of me.

'Pete,' I could hear voices calling to me, 'come back!' But I didn't stop.

I could see the heavenly birds flying past me again, so I knew I must be heading in the right direction. I could feel Perfect Pete returning. This must be the way. I felt my heartbeat quicken. Fuck, was this it? Was I going to be able to get back up? I began to rise but then I lost my grip and slid back down again. I was worried I was going to give myself a heart attack, but at the same time I began to see segments of my old personality returning. I started to remember who I was, as if I'd left all my DNA in heaven and now I was edging back towards it, pulling the fragments back together, mending what had been broken.

'This is the way! This is the way!' I shouted. 'I've found the code to heaven.'

On the journey along the spiral I bumped into this bloke whose face I recognized from Brighton, although

I'd never spoken to him. He had sideburns, bushy, curly hair and a round nose. It was a normal sort of face, but with a bit of a smirk.

'Hello Pete, you all right?' the man asked. I knew I knew him but I couldn't remember his name.

'Who are you?' I asked.

'God.'

'Fucking hell! No way.'

I knew he was telling the truth and that meant I was on the right track. The moment I knew it was the truth we started to float around together in the sky.

'My God, you are God!'

'Anything you'd like to ask me?' he wondered.

'I'd like to know how to get back to heaven.'

His face began to age, becoming decrepit. He had ketamine around his nose and he started to spiral away from me. I was losing my grip, the code was deserting me and I wasn't going to be able to hang on any longer, as my grip weakened I slid back down the spiral, my descent getting faster and faster, like a fairground slide. The good feelings were going, replaced by bad. I was lower than I had ever been, all by myself as I crashed into some barbed wire and nettles, landing in a hostile world full of things that hurt. There were flies and maggots eating at my rotting flesh. It was dark, like the pits of hell. There was a stink of shit. My wrists had been slit open, my blood was pouring out. I'd shat and pissed myself. Zombie-like creatures were rising up around me, moaning and growling, grabbing at me. There was a flock of crows circling in the sky, making ugly cawing noises as they went. My heart seemed to have stopped beating and I was certain I was having a heart attack.

I couldn't remember any of the code at all. It was like it was obscured from me in mud as I slid lower. It was growing darker and darker. I was going down and down and I knew the final stage was going to be to meet Satan. I seemed to be able to see whatever was going to happen next.

Everyone I had ever known was there but they were no longer in a perfect, beautiful state. They'd grown old and decrepit, the complete opposite to how they had looked in heaven. I couldn't look anyone in the eye any more; it was like they all hated me. The feeling of being alone and hated was crushing my brain.

I understood that the spiral was to do with everything in the whole world. I could see a cherry, and every time I rose up the spiral it became ripe and delicious looking, but every time I slipped down it began to shrivel, wrinkle and grow old. The same was happening to the faces of all my friends.

'Pete,' a voice inside me said, 'Pete, you don't want to end like this.'

Suddenly I could see the whole code. I knew how to get up the spiral. I could still save myself from damnation. I began to rise back up, get a little way up then lose sight of the code and feel myself falling again towards hell. I could see pictures from my life as I yo-yoed up and down, gradually scrabbling my way towards the top, as my cherry and my friends grew young and beautiful again. Suddenly I was safe and things clicked back into place.

'Don't you ever try to kill yourself.' God's voice was back. He was showing me a scene with my body lying dead, having followed a different path. 'How dare you? You can't just take away what I have given you.'

'Oh,' I muttered, 'sorry.'

'Louder!'

'SORRY!'

'Stop wanting things you can't have. Accept what you've got. Stop taking drugs. You will never be allowed up here on drugs.'

'OK.'

With every lesson I learnt I would hear a little 'ching-ching' in my head, like a penny dropping, like a fruit machine lining up the cherries, and all the birds would whistle a happy tune. With each lesson learnt I edged further up the spiral – 'ching-ching!' Everyone was looking.

'What do you say?' God boomed.

'Thank you.'

'Louder!'

'THANK YOU!'

I was being given a second chance. He said I could go back to the party.

'Pull your trousers up,' he told me.

I couldn't believe it. I was back with my friends in heaven, struggling hard to stay with it, not to let the code slip away from me. Each time I was able to move up there always seemed to be two paths to choose from, and I kept on choosing the wrong one and would start slipping back towards hell, losing the next bit of the code.

'Pete,' I heard a friend say, 'there's someone here who wants to speak to you. He's trying to get in touch.'

'Really, is it my dad?'

'No.'

I could feel myself slipping again.

'Is it Dave?'

'No.'

Another lurch downwards.

'Oh shit, is it Joolz?'

All the birds burst into song. I'd found the right answer. A black cherry came spiralling down from heaven and connected with my red cherry, sending up a pink and purple spiral. 'Ching-ching!' My whole body felt like Joolz.

'Joolz!'

'All right, mate?'

'Fucking hell, I miss you, man. Can't believe it's you.'

'Shall we sit over there?' he suggested.

'OK.'

We sat down in a field. I could see his shape next to me as we chatted for a bit. He seemed to know all about what had been happening to me and how bad it had been.

'Where are you?' I asked.

'Can't tell you that, mate. Look, I'm here to help you. Watch this.'

I stood up and started walking in the direction he was pointing. Cameras were flashing in my eyes, going off in my face – 'ching-ching, ching-ching, ching-ching'. Voices were cheering and whistling, shouting my name. I was coming out of the *Big Brother* house, doing the walk through the cheering crowd. Mum was there, Alex was there, Dad was there. Billy Idol, Jim Carrey, everyone. Everything had come together. My whole body felt like Perfect Pete again. The pigtails had disappeared and my hair had gone back to my old Mohican. I was a whole person again. I was the winner of the show.

I realized Joolz was telling me that this was the path I had to follow if I wanted to get back to heaven. I had to enter *Big Brother* and I had to win.

The whole scene vanished.

'If you ever need me,' Joolz said, 'do what your mum says and chant Nam Myoho Renge Kyo.'

'OK.'

'I'm looking after you now, so everything is going to be OK. You don't need to worry any more because I'll do all the worrying for you.'

When I arrived back down among my friends I found that I could connect with them again in a way I hadn't been able to do since the New Year. It felt like I had telepathic powers, helping me to go straight into their minds by looking deep into their eyes, without having to say anything. I was able to connect with them instantly and totally in the same way I had done in heaven. All the barriers had lifted and I was back to how I had been before everything started to go wrong. I could talk to people again. I had taken the first step on my journey back to being Perfect Pete again. From then on I knew what I had to do to remember myself. All I had to do now was make sure I fulfilled Joolz's prophecy.

CHAPTER TWENTY-FIVE

BIG BROTHER

Mum was getting settled in France with Alex. She'd been able to buy herself a little fisherman's cottage in Honfleur. It needed a lot of work, like most old places, but she loved it. It needed rewiring, new woodwork and tiles and plaster boarding, and there were a lot of mice and birds' nests to be cleared out. It was costing her a lot of money but it was still really cool. It was in the old part of town, on cobbled streets near the harbour, which was full of bobbing fishing boats. It was the whole idyllic scene, like one of those 'find your dream house' television programmes, a million miles from the violence and traffic of the Well Hall Road. She'd found a little music school nearby to teach in and had joined the local choir.

I went over to visit her and found she had made all these local friends already, fishermen and other people with lives that had nothing to do with the music business, with street theatre or with anything in her past. It was a whole new life, a whole new family. I was so pleased to see her happy.

She had put together a big meal with roast lamb and everything and invited her new friends to meet me. Everyone got completely wasted on Calvados and played a drinking game called 'Trou Normand' which ended up with Gilles, one of her best friends, falling off the chair he was standing on, smack across the table, smashing everything except the glass in his hand. Wow! These people really knew how to party!

Mum's little two-year-old adopted niece, Julia, spent the whole day solemnly watching me. By the evening she was able to bang her chest and intone 'wankeurs' in a cute French accent. Wicked, man. Perfect Pete goes global!

Despite all the positive changes, Mum still had to work in the local McDonald's just to generate enough money for her and Alex to live on while she got the house finished and habitable. I could see she was really stressed out, which made me feel stressed as well. It didn't seem fair that she was still doing menial jobs like that after everything she had been through and everything she had done for us. Life should have been starting to get easier for her.

She looked so exhausted from all the years of struggle and I was still going to have to borrow some money off her just to get back home to England, because I was even broker than she was, so I wasn't being any help.

I felt terrible for her. I wanted to find a way to make some money to sort her out. I wanted not to be a worry to her any more, to find a way to make her more comfortable and to be completely independent, like a proper grown-up son.

If the vision in heaven proved to be right and I did get to win *Big Brother* that would sort it for all of us. I had to win; there was no choice. If I didn't then the whole thing would be a lie and I would never be able to get back to heaven, never get to see Joolz again and never be able to make any money to help Mum.

I finally got round to cutting off my pigtails, feeling ready to start saying goodbye once and for all to Pigtail Pete, as I continued my journey back to being Perfect Pete.

As well as getting back to working on my music and my cartoons, I was starting to think about studying comedy. I'd always liked making people laugh, even when sometimes I'd known they were laughing at the Tourette's more than anything I was saying. Right from the early days when I was told I reminded someone of Charlie Chaplin, I'd known I could do the whole comic timing thing. Maybe it's like having a musical ear. Sometimes I could even channel the Tourette's to deliberately help me get a laugh. A well-timed raspberry seldom fails to raise a smile. I wanted to learn more about the craft of comedy, just as I'd learnt about the craft of using a studio with Dave, and learnt art at school and college. There was a lot of comedy in my Daddy Fantastic persona, as well as in the cartoons I'd been doing ever since I was a kid. I was sure there was something there I could work on. A tourettey comedian – why not? Comedy can come from a million different places, from Chaplin's walk to Carrey's mugging, from Robin Williams's stream-of-consciousness babble to Eddie Izzard's surreal, transvestite, genius ramblings. Humour lurks in some of the darkest corners of people's experiences, from Richard Pryor's drug addiction to Stephen Fry's manic depression. People who have travelled to other places can return with stories to entertain those who have never been forced to make the same journeys.

I enrolled in a comedy course being run in The Laines in Brighton, eager to find out whatever I could, to hone another skill. It was fun. We all sat around in a circle, playing a sort of *Whose Line is it Anyway?* game, improvising comedy and learning the tricks of the trade. The others laughed at me a lot and seemed to like my ideas. It felt like a good place to be.

A friend I'd met in Brighton, called Juan, had seen an item on the *Richard and Judy Show* about Eye-Q tablets, which are a mixture of fish oils and evening primrose oil. It's all about omega oils and natural fatty acids which are thought to help with all sorts of things like vision, coordination, learning ability, memory and concentration. They were supposed to help people like me who felt they had a sort of mist in their heads. This mist had always made it too easy for my attention to wander, making proper conversation difficult. If people tried to talk to me it would seem to them that I wasn't listening, wasn't able to follow the thread. Maybe the tablets replace some missing chemicals in the brain or mend some broken electrical connection. Who knows? It seemed worth a try. I bought a pot of the Eye-Q tablets and within a couple of months of taking them I found that I was able to concentrate on what people were saying to me, able to follow sentences right to the end, like I was coming out of the clouds. I rang Mum immediately.

'Mum, Mum,' I shouted excitedly. 'I can talk again. It's wicked.'

We had a proper conversation for the first time in ages, with me able to say all the things I was planning to say, only occasionally interrupting myself. I've taken them every day since then and everyone who has problems even remotely like mine should try them. I dare say they won't work for everyone, and no one knows for sure why they do work for some of us, but who cares about the whys and what ifs as long as there's a chance they will help? End of commercial break.

The initial auditions for *Big Brother* are massive cattle markets, millions of hopeful people being shunted around the place as the producers desperately try to sift through them and narrow their options down to manageable levels. I queued for what felt like five hours before I got my turn to jump in front of the camera and show them as much of my personality as I could in thirty seconds. I leapt straight in, determined to be completely myself.

'Hi, I'm Perfect Pete!'

I didn't hold in anything, just let it all out, being myself, feeling comfortable, letting them see who I really was, not even trying to keep the Tourette's cooped up inside. I exploded in front of the cameras and let it all rip, pouring out whatever came into my head, letting the tics fall where they chose, trusting to my instincts for timing. If so many people in Brighton liked the real Perfect Pete, maybe Big Brother would as well.

'OK,' Big Brother said, smiling, 'you can drop the act now, Pete.'

'No,' I said. 'You don't understand. It's not an act. I've got Tourette's. This is me. This is how I am.'

I noticed that a woman with a clipboard stuck a star next to my name on the list. I asked her about it later and she denied it, but I saw her do it and it made me feel like I was doing the right thing. I was growing sure that this time it was going to work, that the vision was going to be proved true. This time I was going to get in and I was going to win and I was going to be able to find my way back to heaven just like Joolz had shown me.

I'd learnt now how to stick up for myself a bit in the confrontational exercises. Living in Brighton and all the experiences I'd had there had taught me a few tricks, helped me to overcome my fear of standing up to people. I still don't like it and I will always try to avoid any sort of stand-off or argument or fight, but I could at least pretend to do it enough to get through the auditions. I came away feeling really positive, but not daring to be certain, having failed before. If you build your hopes too high the chances are you are going to take a tumble.

Mum received a phone call from a psychiatrist doing assessments on whether potential contestants were up to the job.

'When he was asked about his father,' the psychiatrist told her, 'Pete said he was "mental". What exactly would you understand him to mean by that?'

'Oh he didn't mean mental,' Mum assured him, worried that Big Brother might think insanity ran in the family, 'as in mentally unstable. It's just a word he uses about things or people when he finds them entertaining or eccentric or exciting. Like he might say "wicked" without meaning that something was actually evil.'

By the end of the call she had no more clues as to whether or not I was going to be accepted. Weeks after the first audition it was my turn to get the phone call.

'Hello Pete,' the voice said, 'would you like to be a *Big Brother* housemate?'

'Oh, yeah!'

Then everything became a rush and a blur of new experiences and new faces. I was whisked off to a secret location in Belgium for two weeks to keep me away from the media and from the other housemates, before being brought back to the house for the entrance ceremony and first-time meetings. Big Brother was now in control of everything, and that felt nice. I didn't have to make any difficult decisions, or even any easy ones. They made them all for me. They took over the running of my life and all I had to do was be myself – my speciality.

My friends in Brighton weren't too sure I'd made the right decision. *Big Brother*, reality television, it all smelt like a bit of a sell-out to them. I could see their point of view – I usually can see other people's points of view, which can be a bit difficult sometimes when you're trying to work out what is best for you – but I instinctively knew it was the right thing for me to do. Even before Joolz told me it was the way I had to go, I'd known I would feel comfortable in the house. It's all performing, isn't it? Whether it's a reality TV show, dancing in a gay trance club in Brighton, or performing on a street corner in Covent Garden, it's all the same, just different venues, different media. Just because *Big Brother* was watched and liked by millions of people, not just by passers-by in the street, didn't make it any less valid as a platform for Perfect Pete to do his thing.

* * *

Arriving at the *Big Brother* house felt like one giant tourettey twitch, a huge buzzy bear hug feeling of finally having reached my destiny. When I climbed out of the car backwards and turned to face the crowd it was like I was coming home. The Tourette's and I were one as I spun and gurned, camped and prat-fell my way through the tunnels of barriers that held back the hordes of fans who were there for a show without even knowing anything about the players. It all passed by in a daze of crowds and flashbulbs going off all around. It was like the whole area was my own stage and I was the master of it, performing on automatic pilot, just following my instincts. They cheered and laughed and shouted, egging me on to greater and greater heights. Freddy Mercury, the genie from Aladdin, Tourette-boy, the bedroom radio DJ and old Monkey-face from the school playground came together in one orgasmic explosion as I strung the moment out for as long as I possibly could before disappearing in through the doors. For a second Davina was afraid I was going to go on for too long, that I was risking stretching the crowd's patience too far and would end up looking like a bit of a show-off and be receiving boos instead of cheers, but the crowd stayed with me. They seemed to enjoy the act, to like what they saw. Even though they had no idea who I was or why I was acting the way I was, they seemed willing to indulge me in order to see what would come next.

What came next was a spectacular pratfall down the stairs into the house, beamed into millions of homes simultaneously.

'Fucking hell,' they must all have been saying from their armchairs and sofas around the country. 'What the fuck was that?'

As I came through into the main room of the house and met my first housemate, Bonnie, I felt a huge sense of relief, like I'd finally been able to scratch an itch that had been bothering me for years. I'd arrived. I was safe. I was inside the house, at least for a few weeks and hopefully for the full three months. I had reached the next stage of my journey back to heaven.

I liked pretty much everyone in there, but as the weeks passed I began to form some strong friendships. Nikki seemed a bit slow at first, a bit head-in-the-clouds, a bit of a bimbo. She came in wearing a bunny outfit because she'd just been to a hen party or something, and she looked a lot better once she was out of that. I liked Lea and Dickie the most. They seemed to be more mature than the rest, more open to life's experiences. I felt I had more in common with them. Lisa seemed good fun to start with, but then she kept worrying about whether I was all right with her, which I totally was, except when she kept going on about it. Then Lea started going on about how I'd changed towards her, which I didn't think

I had at all. I was so fed up with bringing out this reaction in people. I couldn't understand why they couldn't just accept me as I was without all the worry and anxiety. The world is full of potential bunny-boilers, and it gets on my nerves sometimes. I try to be the same with everyone all the time, try to be kind, try to be friendly, try to be fun. The rest is just bollocks going on inside their heads.

I've never liked answering questions. I can never find the answers in time and it makes me start touretting all over the place as I struggle to look for them and not let the questioner down. But the diary room in the house wasn't so bad, maybe because there wasn't anyone there looking at me, just a camera. I'm very comfortable with cameras. I can't explain why, I just always have been. Big Brother still asked some questions that I found hard, like, 'How would you like to be remembered?' Do people really carry around ready-made answers to questions like that?

When I first went in I felt totally confident that I would win because of seeing it happen in my vision and hearing Joolz's words, but as the weeks went past I began to lose my nerve. Everyone else in the house seemed to be so much more interesting than me, so much better at joining in conversations, with so much more to say for themselves. I could imagine that the viewers would be getting bored of me because I couldn't talk about stuff. Most of what the others talked about seemed to be shit to me anyway. They were always gossiping about one another, that sort of thing, and I couldn't think of anything worth saying half the time, which worried me.

But then I kept being given little signs, which seemed to be telling me that everything was going to be all right. The moment I walked into the house I noticed that there was a spiral logo on the dining-room door that seemed to suggest I was going in the right direction. Then a bloke actually called Spiral came in, making it seem even more like a definite sign. The furniture was all in the same pink and blue colours that I had seen in heaven. When Mikey came in I found out he had 'God is love' tattooed on his chest. When we talked he told me he had met Him as well.

Outside the house there was a tree filled with birds, which was exactly as I had been shown in the vision. It all felt completely right.

Richard wanted to cut my hair one day.

'Let me give you a Mohi,' he said.

So we did it in the kitchen and when he'd finished it was exactly the same style I'd had when I was Perfect Pete, I couldn't believe it.

'Perfect, Pete,' he exclaimed when he'd finished, without having any idea that had once been my nickname. I felt like I'd taken another giant step back to being the Perfect Pete I had once been.

The barbecue was a brilliant drum kit, and when I started to play it one day I noticed a long hair at the back of it, curled into the shape of the word 'Pete'. Then I found a bird shit with the number 23 appearing in the middle. Then another day Spiral wore a jumper with the number 23 on it. When I was in the shower during the last week some of the shampoo fell on the floor and when I looked down it was forming into the shapes of exploding fireworks, like the ones I knew they always let off when they announced the winner. That seemed like another good omen.

Lea was always telling me that I was going to win. 'When you do,' she told me one day, 'you'll leave the house wearing orange.'

Her words worried me a little because I knew I didn't have anything orange with me. A few days later Mikey and I swapped some clothes and I suddenly realized he had given me an orange top. Even though I didn't wear it on the day in the end, it put my mind at rest to have it.

I was outside the house with Nikki on another day, talking about birds, and suddenly one shat on my head, which seemed to me like a direct signal. All these signs made me feel I was being watched by the people in heaven and they were giving me little encouragements to keep me going.

Despite all these signs, I had no way of knowing what was going on in the outside world, no way of knowing what the newspapers were saying about us, who they were backing and who they were putting down. I had no way of knowing if the viewers liked me or hated me.

In my low moments I began to panic. What if I didn't win? I could hardly bear to think about it. It would mean my whole future couldn't happen. I would never be able to get back to heaven. It would mean the meeting with Joolz had just been in my mind, that it had never happened and everything I'd been talking about was bullshit. Mum would still be broke and I would just be another ex-druggie, touretting freak on the streets of Brighton. I didn't know what I would do if that happened. But nor did I know what I could do differently to make sure I won. I could only be myself. I couldn't pretend to be anything I wasn't. I just had to trust in my own visions and the power of the Buddhist chanting. I just had to trust Joolz. There were times when I felt very low.

I didn't realize how much I liked and fancied Nikki till she was evicted from the house and suddenly wasn't there any more. I missed cuddling her. I missed the affection. I knew she really liked me because she was always pouncing on me, and I secretly liked that, but I didn't realize how much until she had gone.

I was also missing the ketamine, dreaming about it a lot, longing for it. I would dream I was going down to Brighton with Joolz and the others, but I knew when I was awake that I couldn't go back down that path now. I had to give up drugs and follow the path that God and Joolz had showed me.

*　*　*

When the moment approached for Davina to make the final announcement of who had won, I really didn't have any idea what was going to happen next. I truly thought that Glyn would probably win because he was always so cheerful and had had such a perfect life so far. He was a local boy made good with none of the darkness that lurks inside me, plotting to take over. I don't know what I would have done if that had happened. The moment she announced that it was me the whole vision came true, just as Joolz had predicted, just as I had seen in heaven. It was all true. It was all right, just like I'd been told. Everything had come full circle.

I screamed my head off in a mixture of excitement, relief, happiness and Tourette's. I didn't know what to do, so I rampaged around the room, the Tourette's searching for an outlet for all the energy pent up inside me.

When the doors of the house opened to let me out my vision was waiting for me on the other side. It was exactly as Joolz had showed me. There were screaming crowds and fireworks lighting up the night sky. I saw Mum and Alex, and Davina. There was so much noise and it was all good. I tripped and rolled down the stairs into the crowd, shaking hands as I went, shouting and ticcing and totally joyful. From now on everything was going to be wicked. It was mental.

EPILOGUE

Emerging back out into the real world was like, Wow, man! It was like coming out of prison or returning from a prolonged stop-over in outer space. It felt like I needed another dose of independence training just to work out what to do next. For more than three months we'd been locked away from the world, completely looked after and institutionalized. I had no idea what the viewing public thought of me or what had been going on while I was inside. Had I embarrassed my friends and family, or made them proud? I'd had the letter from Mum in the house, which had been positive, but then she was bound to be on my side because she was my mum. What about everyone else? I guessed the reaction couldn't be anything too bad or I wouldn't have won, but I had no idea to what level viewers had come to accept the Tourette's symptoms.

It was a shock to find that everyone I met was being so nice to me. Everyone appeared to want to help me in any way they could. Some of them seemed a bit fake, like they

were only doing their jobs with fixed smiles and big prom-
ises, but most of them seemed to be genuinely friendly and
keen to give me the best advice possible, to protect me
from all the bad stuff, steer me through the celebrity mine-
field and help me to make the most of my good luck.

I was even left a message from God over the Internet,
congratulating me on winning. 'I knew you'd win,' He
wrote, 'but then again, I do know everything.'

The trouble was there was just so much to take in,
so many offers, so many demands, and so many messages from people. Over the following few days I tried to
reacclimatize myself and to work out exactly what was
going on. If I went out into the street everyone would
recognize me instantly, crowding round, being friendly
and giving me things. If people shouted at me from passing cars or windows it was messages of support, greet-
ings or jokes. The taunts and abuse and suspicion
seemed to have melted magically away. Mostly they just
wanted to shout 'wankers' like it was a comedy catchphrase, or to say hi and tell me they'd enjoyed the show.
It was all so incredibly cool. It was great, but it was dis-
orientating because it had all happened so suddenly,
with no build-up and no warning.

I discovered we'd managed to raise around £400,000
for the Tourette's Syndrome Association which made me
feel proud. Lots of parents of children with Tourette's
were speaking up and saying how much me being on
television had helped their kids to be accepted by other

people. Through getting to know me on the screen, people seemed to have realized that just because someone shouts a swear word in the street, or does some horrendous tic, doesn't mean they're mad or dangerous or deserve a good kicking. It just means they have an illness, like someone with a limp or a cough. I was told that in playgrounds all over the country kids were actually whistling, banging their chests and shouting 'wankers!' as a mark of respect, a bit like saying 'give me five' or 'Eezamanna'. Kids who had previously been bullied were now respected for being 'like Pete on *Big Brother*'. This was an added bonus that I'd never expected – Tourette's was cool at last. Who would have believed it was possible?

In her letter Mum had told me that Dad had promised he would be there to cheer when I came out. She'd tried to persuade him not to change his mind and to make my vision complete if I won (well, complete apart from Billy Idol and Jim Carrey turning up, of course). For a while it looked like he might be going to do it, but in the end he decided not to. I wasn't mega-surprised. He didn't want it to look like he was jumping on a bandwagon and only showing an interest because of the show. I could understand that. There was so much going on, and so many people talking to me at once, I was distracted from my disappointment. It would have been nice to see him again though.

* * *

Even the guys in Brighton seemed to have come to terms with the idea of me being in *Big Brother* and didn't see it as so much of a sell-out any more. Maybe they had watched a bit of it and seen that I hadn't changed, that I was still the same bloke. They seemed to be willing to forgive me and were keen to get Daddy Fantastic back on the road. Someone told me the Daddy Fantastic website had had about four million hits while I was in the house – that's the scary power of telly. Nimbus the Noodle's girlfriend, Madame Pussycat, had become their manager and had made all sorts of plans for us to go on the road as soon as I came out of the house.

The problem for me was that everyone wanted me to do everything and there wasn't enough time to fit it all in. On top of that my relationship with Nikki seemed to suddenly be of enormous interest to every tabloid and magazine writer in the world. I couldn't believe how many times I was reading that we were going to be together for life, that we were splitting up, and everything else in between. They predicted when we would marry, how many kids we would have, even what genders they would be. Hang on! We'd only been an item for a couple of weeks, only known each other three months. We hadn't even met one another's families or friends.

The magazines were wanting me to pose for photo shoots with Nikki and the publishers were wanting me to write this book really quickly. On top of all that I was contacted by Guy Chambers, who wanted to work with me on some of my songs. Guy is a bit of a legend in the music business. He's the man who wrote 'Angels' and a load of other hits for Robbie Williams. He's also written with or for just about every other big name in the industry.

While we were working together I rented a flat in London that used to belong to Adam Ant – how weird is that? But that isn't the only coincidence. Guy studied at the Guildhall, like Mum, and his first group, The Burmoe Brothers, actually had Marc Almond in the line-up for one of their songs. Guy had also been part of a folk-rock group called The Waterboys, which I had always loved. Mum and Dave had their album when they first fell in love and played it all the time. Everything and everyone, it seems, is cosmically linked somehow.

It was impossible to get my head round it all. There just weren't enough hours in the day and everyone seemed to think that I was spending too much time doing the wrong things. There were some moments that were unbelievably great, like when I was able to give Mum a cheque to write off all her debts, so she didn't have to worry any more about keeping a roof over her and Alex's heads, or even contemplate having to go back behind the fryers in McDonald's. I felt so proud to be able to do that after everything she had done for me and all the sacrifices she had made.

Other moments weren't so good. When it became obvious I wasn't going to be able to tour with them, the guys in Daddy Fantastic went back to thinking I was selling out and letting them down. I felt really bad that they were feeling like that, but I just didn't seem to be able to please everyone at the same time. I got the same sick feeling in my stomach I used to get when I let a goal through at school and the team would yell abuse at me and tell me how badly I'd let them down. I didn't want to let anyone down. I wanted to have a go at everything. I wanted to enjoy the moment and to be with as many of my friends as I could manage for as much time as I could. But it was just impossible, man, and their anger weighed heavily on my heart.

A surprising number of people had come forward with stories to sell to the media about spending nights of drug-fuelled fetish passion with me which I don't have any memory of. Other stories came from people I had always thought were really good friends, which made me confused and unsure who I could trust. Some people told the papers that they knew for sure that I was really gay, usually basing this conclusion on the fact that they had seen me fooling around at parties with drag queen friends and other poofs. There were tales of three-in-a-bed romps and girls being frightened by my perverted sexual demands and massive schlong. I was beginning to wonder if I had a secret life even I didn't know about.

The pressure was building and building. Nikki was wanting me to commit to her for all eternity when we hardly knew each other, and the media kept announcing that we were getting married or breaking up, that my Mum loved Nikki or hated her. They wanted to know every detail of our sex lives, apparently worried that poor petite Nikki wouldn't be able to cope with my monstrous willy, which was growing more terrifyingly enormous with every new story. The rumours and gossip seemed to change every few hours. It was like living at the centre of a hurricane, hundreds of thousands of words and pictures on every newsstand, spinning out of control, and I found myself feeling anxious and guilty when I should have been feeling elated and excited by all the good things that were happening for me.

When we were in the house together Nikki and I were really strongly attracted to one another, but we were living in a completely unnatural environment in there. It was a bit like one of those holiday romances that suddenly seem so very different once you get back home. She can be so funny and adorable and sweet, and I had been swept off my feet. She was always really good at laughing at herself. She would try so hard to listen and learn whenever anyone criticized her.

Once we were released into the outside world, back with our friends and relatives, the gap between our two lifestyles became glaringly obvious. In a way we were still living the same lives because we were doing all the magazine interviews together, appearing on things like the *Jonathan Ross Show*, and Nikki was being rushed around making her *Princess Nikki* television series, but that wasn't enough to cover up the cracks. When we were being just a couple with friends it was obvious we came from very different worlds.

It took me ages to pluck up the courage to tell her about the doubts I was having and to suggest that maybe we could go back just to being good friends. I'm always so bad at that sort of thing, never wanting to upset anyone, always trying to please everyone. It's obvious I will never be able to please everyone now and I'm just going to have to get used to the idea that for every person who likes Perfect Pete, there may be someone who doesn't and the chances are I'm going to have read all about that person's views in a magazine somewhere. That's hard to get my head round.

As soon as I broke up with Nikki all her fans got angry and a lot of them wrote to tell me what a bastard I was. Newspaper journalists immediately joined in the hunt, quoting Nikki as complaining about my unreasonably high sex drive and bizarre sexual preferences.

I realized I'd disappointed all the people who had enjoyed the romance of it all on their screens. But now Cherry is back in my life and she feels the same way about me as I have felt about her for ages. It seems like I'm taking another step towards my goal of returning to heaven. All the time I am getting closer and closer to normality, finally back to being the real Perfect Pete.

This getting famous thing is great, really wicked, but it's not always as easy as it looks from the outside. But that's cool, because it's been a laugh and overall I now love life even more than before. It's all wicked, man.

PETE

The Gallery

THE SCREAMING MAN

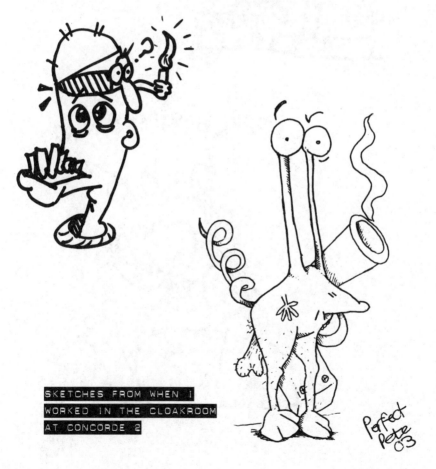

SKETCHES FROM WHEN I
WORKED IN THE CLOAKROOM
AT CONCORDE 2

OTTO THE GARBAGE
MAN!